TIBET
LHASA ➤ KATHMANDU

西藏 00752

APA PUBLICATIONS

Dear Visitor!

Mesmerizing burgundy-robed monks chanting ancient sutras, the world's tallest mountains, ancient sacred routes, exquisite palaces, fabled monasteries – Tibet is all these and more. Perched on a high mountain plateau, this myth-shrouded land offers the traveller a trove of treasures almost impossible to describe because they are so alien to common experiences. Inundate your senses with impressions that will be recalled long after details of particular Buddha images, murals and monasteries are forgotten, and experience the unique welding of Tibet's people and their religion.

 Steve Van Beek, writer and veteran traveller of Asia, was full of anticipation and dread when Tibet first opened its doors to visitors in 1986. 'Had the past been bulldozed and buried by the present?' Van Beek wondered. It was with relief that he found Tibet – although considerably altered by Chinese occupation – much as he had hoped it would be. Landmarks had been demolished and twisting lanes replaced by broad boulevards, but the resilient Tibetan culture was essentially intact. The rarefied air that had permeated the Tibetan monasteries in Kathmandu here pervaded the entire country.

Designed for visitors flying into Lhasa and travelling overland to Kathmandu, this book can also be used if you're making the trip in reverse. In the first part of the book, Van Beek has crafted itineraries which cover the sights in Lhasa. In the second section, he takes you along on short forays into Central Tibet before plunging you into the overland trip to Kathmandu. Be forewarned: while a visit to Tibet can be exhilirating, it can also be difficult. Facilities are often very basic, and altitude sickness may be your biggest problem. Yet, overcome these obstacles and you will find Tibet an adventure few regions in the world can equal.

Hans Höfer
Publisher, Insight Guides

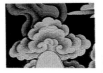

C O N T E N T S

Pages 2/3:
the southern route
via Gyantse

Pages 8/9:
Tashilhunpo Monastery
in Shigatse

'Rooftop of the World', the sobriquet given to Tibet, alludes not only to its extreme altitude but also to the isolation which has contributed to the creation of its unique culture. Tibet's lofty perch high above the hurly-burly of the lowlands has shaped its other-worldly attitudes and discouraged even hardy colonists from establishing a toehold.

Living at an average elevation of 5,000m (15,000ft) above sea level, a vast and arid high desert plateau hemmed in by the two mountain ranges of the world's highest peaks, the Tibetans are people of the cold, high desert: austere, pragmatic, tenacious, independent, pious, diligent, cohesive, xenophobic, occasionally fierce, yet taciturn and shy.

Early Folklore

Legend says that Tibet was once covered by the ocean, an interesting concordance with geologic history, which has Tibet lapped by the seas before the Indian tectonic plate collided with the Asian mainland and pushed Tibet to its present dizzying heights.

In the Yarlung Valley southeast of Lhasa, the briny waters receded, revealing two of the most unlikely candidates for a marriage: a monkey and a fierce ogress. Contrary to Western belief, the monkey represented not mischief but wisdom. Buddhism, which did not appear until eons later, regarded the ape as the manifestation of the Bodhisattva of Compassion, Chenrezig (Avalokiteshvara). The ogress was a wretched creature given to howling from treetops. She was ostracised for her crude nature but Chenrezig took pity on her and the couple produced six offspring. With time, the children lost all simian characteristics to become the Tibetan race.

Himalaya, birthplace of the gods

Statue of Songtsen Gampo

Tibet's first monarch was a stranger who appeared one day in the Yarlung Valley. When the Tibetans asked where he came from, the stranger pointed over his shoulder to indicate India. The awe-struck Tibetans thought he meant he had descended from the sky. Mistaking him for some divine being sent by the gods, they promptly proclaimed him as their king.

First Emperor

The 33rd king of the Yarlung line, Songtsen Gampo (AD620–650), was the first ruler to be recorded in Tibetan history, simply because one of his ministers devised a written script for the Tibetan language. During Songtsen Gampo's reign, Tibet not only initiated trade contacts with China, India, Nepal and the lands to the west, but also began expanding its borders. The Chinese and Nepalese sought to curtail imperial ambitions by creating alliances sealed with that all-purpose diplomatic glue: a wife. China dispatched Princess Wencheng and from Nepal came Princess Bhrikuti to join the king's three Tibetan wives. The pair of queens brought with them a new religion – Buddhism.

Until then, the Tibetans had followed a fundamental religion which attempted to reconcile the place of humankind in heaven and earth. It soon developed into a form of animism which postulated the existence of spirits in trees, rocks and mountains. Elaborate propitiation rituals were developed to quell malevolent spirits and encourage benevolent spirits to serve human needs. Called Bon (pronounced Bone), the religion has survived in scattered pockets in Tibet and Nepal to the present day and, now, has become largely intertwined with Tibetan Buddhism. Bon's most obvious manifestations are the practice of circumambulating anticlockwise, the opposite to Buddhism, placing stone cairns on hilltops, and the flying of blue, white, red, yellow and green pennants from housetops.

11

Prayer flags crown a mountain pass

While the adoption of Buddhism was a landmark event, Songtsen Gampo's court seemed to have done little more than dabble in it. Buddhism was to languish and be banned for a period after his death but during his reign, Songtsen Gampo moved his court to Lhasa and erected a modest palace on Red Hill, now occupied by the Potala. He also constructed a number of temples across Tibet, including the Jokhang and the Ramoche to house Buddha images brought to Tibet by each of his foreign queens.

Buddhism Established

Trisong Detsen (755–797) continued the work of his predecessor, expanding Tibet's borders to incorporate major portions of Central Asia and made Tibet nearly twice as large as it is today. During his reign, interest in Buddhism was revived.

Two Indian Buddhists teachers, Guru Rinpoche (Padmasambhava) and Santarakshita, were invited to establish Tibet's first Buddhist monastery. A handsome edifice rose at Samye in the Yarlung Valley and the first Tibetan Buddhist monks were trained and ordained. To promote the religion, Trisong Detsen ordered noble families to support the monasteries, a decree repellent to Bon-worshippers, who ultimately sowed the seeds for Buddhism's demise.

Buddhism prospered during subsequent reigns with great tomes of Buddhist scriptures translated into Tibetan during the rule of Repachen (815–838). Opposition to the religion had been growing, however, and culminated in a backlash of fury that led to the murder of Repachen. His successor, Langdarma, banned the religion, persecuting its adherents until he was assassinated six years later by a recalcitrant monk.

Internecine fighting reduced not just Buddhism but the entire empire to anarchy and chaos as Tibet entered a Dark Age that would last for 200 years. By 899, the empire had fragmented into warring feudal states. Buddhism was preserved only because a few monks fled to West Tibet and to the eastern state of Kham and continued to propagate it there. Central Tibet was once again the domain of Bon worshippers.

Atisha Arrives

In 1042, the Mahayana teacher Atisha journeyed from India to lecture in West Tibet at the invitation of its king. Under his tutelage, Buddhism began a slow climb back to its former prominence. Like the scattered kingdoms, Buddhism functioned as a patchwork of diverse doctrines with nearly 20 distinct sects, each isolated from the other. Eventually, four principal orders emerged and vied for pre-eminence: the Nyingmapa, Kagyudpa, Sakyapa and Kadampa, which later evolved into the Gelugpa (Virtuous Ones).

In 1247, the Mongols appointed a Sakya Monastery scholar, Sakya Pundit, as the ruler of Tibet, thereby establishing the monastery as a centre of Tibetan power. Sakya continued to provide the nation's leaders until 1354 when they were overthrown. In the melee that followed, no single sect was able to assert control and once again the country disintegrated into warring factions.

Eventually, one order prevailed over the rest. The Gelugpa was founded in the 15th century by the great religious reformer, Tsongkhapa, and grew steadily in power. Its leaders established important monasteries at Chamdo, Drepung, Ganden, Sera and Tashilhunpo, which became vital centres of learning, culture and art. The Gelugpa are sometimes referred to as the Yellow Hat sect by outsiders for their headgear, distinguishing them from the other Red Hat sects. Both terms are misleading and simplistic.

The Glorious Fifth

Seeking to wield political influence, the powerful Gelugpa abbot of Drepung, Sonam Gyatso, sought support from the Mongols, who responded by naming him the Dalai Lama and giving him authority over the whole of Tibet. By their act, they established the U (Central) region around Lhasa as the government for the country and cre-

A Ganden monk with his rosary

ated an institution of religious political leaders which has survived to this day. Aside from a brief resurgence of Nyingmapa rule in the mid-17th century, the U region held the reins of power.

The next great historical figure was the Fifth Dalai Lama (1617–82), a Gelugpa abbot often referred to as the Great Fifth. A formidable leader and a visionary, he ruled a realm that encompassed territory from Mount Kailas to the Kham region. On Lhasa's Red Hill where Songtsen Gampo had built his palace, he began the construction of a massive citadel that would serve both as an administrative and a religious centre: the Potala Palace.

So large was the Great Fifth's influence in unifying the country and so competent and cohesive the band of administrators he assembled that his death in 1682 was kept secret for 12 years until the completion of the Potala.

In China, the Manchus had ousted the Ming emperors in 1644 and had begun to court the Fifth Dalai Lama and other Tibetan notables. After an amicable visit to China by the Dalai Lama in 1652, relations soured. In 1705, the Manchus induced a Mongol prince to invade Tibet and occupy Lhasa. The Sixth Dalai Lama, reputed to have been more fond of women and wine than his duties, was sent to China but died en route. Despite incursions by Dzungar Mongols – who came as saviours and ended as sackers of religious sites – the Chinese maintained suzerainty over Tibet, ruling through *ambans*, or governors, who exercised their authority through Tibetan leaders but left few doubts about who was really in charge.

The Dalai Lamas who succeeded the Great Fifth were unexceptional men in an unremarkable age. A number of them died or were disposed of before reaching maturity and were thus unable to exert much influence. It fell to the 13th Dalai Lama who came to power in 1895 to deal with a new threat – Western colonisation.

The great monastery of Drepung

The Great Game

By the turn of the century, Tibet had acquired new significance in Western, notably British, eyes. Britain became concerned that Russia was concluding a Tibetan alliance. This was viewed as detrimental to British interests in the Great Game being played out for territorial control of Central Asia. Accordingly, the British marched into Tibet to force a treaty upon the Dalai Lama. The expedition, led by Col. Francis Younghusband in 1904, met token resistance south of Gyantse. Displaying a singular lack of judgment, the British soldiers opened fire, killing 700 Tibetans within minutes. They acquired their treaty but alarmed the Chinese, who tightened their hold over the country.

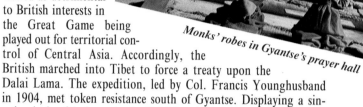

Monks' robes in Gyantse's prayer hall

The overthrow of the Manchus in 1911 stalled Chinese ambitions in Tibet while China dealt with its own internal problems. At the Simla Conference of 1914, the Tibetans tried to assert their independence but were rebuffed by the British, who granted them autonomy under Chinese overlordship, an arrangement that pleased neither party.

In 1949, the Communists took power in China and near the top of their agenda was the incorporation of Tibet into the Chinese polity. In 1950, Chinese armies invaded eastern Tibet, overcoming fierce resistance. In 1951, the Chinese government granted Tibet autonomy in its domestic affairs but garrisoned troops there.

Chinese Occupation

Chinese occupation chafed and in 1956, political agitation against its presence began. Chinese soldiers took over Lhasa and confrontations escalated. In 1959, the Dalai Lama fled to India, eventually taking up residence in Dharmasala. From this base, he has for over 30 years provided guidance to the expatriate Tibetan communities spread throughout India and the world, and to Tibetans in Tibet who continue to revere him.

After 1960, the Chinese policy was to suppress Tibetan institutions, eradicating all symbols of the past. Much of the destruction of monasteries began after 1959 with images and artefacts sold in the antique markets of Hong Kong or melted down to pad Beijing's coffers. In 1965, the Chinese established Tibet as an Autonomous Region ruled by Beijing. At the same time, they carved away portions of its territory, creating the province of Xizang and adding land to existing Chinese provinces.

The Cultural Revolution from 1966 to 1976 was particularly harsh on Tibetans. Systematic persecution reportedly killed hundreds of thousands of Tibetans and senseless destruction of the religious sites reduced the number of monasteries from 2,463 in 1959 to a mere 10 by 1976, according to a Chinese estimate.

Recognising the excesses of these years and as partial atonement for the damage, since 1980, the Chinese have restored many of the old monasteries and trained Tibetan artists to create new Buddha images. They have also relaxed many of the strictures, giving Tibetans a greater hand in planning their own lives. However, period military crackdowns continue to threaten their limited freedom.

Teachings of the Buddha

Tibetan Mahayana Buddhism is a rich, multi-faceted, multi-tiered religion followed by most Tibetans regardless of status. Its multiplicity of deity manifestations perform a specific function and appeal to simple worshippers whose devotion is focused on pilgrimages, prayer and offerings. At the same time, Tibetan Buddhism's comprehensive theology embodies sophisticated philosophical treatises that challenge scholars with complex concepts.

The religion's founder, a prince named Siddhartha Gautama, was born about 543BC in Lumbini, Nepal. He left the palace grounds at the age of 29 where he lived in cocooned and cossetted luxury. So appalled was he by the sight of an old man, a cripple and a corpse when he was finally able to leave the palace that he abandoned his privileged family and wandered from place to place to seek a solution to suffering.

Prince Siddhartha achieved enlightenment in Bodhgaya near Benares, India, meditating beneath a *pipal* tree, oblivious to all distractions and temptations. Worshipped as Sakyamuni, the Buddha of the Present, he declared one must follow the Middle Way and reject extremes of pleasure and pain. He preached

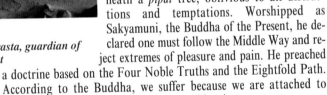

Dhritarasta, guardian of the East

a doctrine based on the Four Noble Truths and the Eightfold Path. According to the Buddha, we suffer because we are attached to people and things in a world where nothing is permanent.

Buddhism teaches that one can do away with suffering by ridding oneself of desire through discipline and meditation. Buddhists believe that the 'self' is nothing but an illusion trapped in the endless cycle of *samsara*, or rebirth, and created by *karma*, the chain of cause and effect. By following the Buddhist *dharma*, or teachings, one can escape the cycle and achieve *nirvana*, considered as essentially the extinction of the ego.

Spring comes to Gyama valley

Interwoven into Tibetan Buddhism is the influence of the Tantric cults, a legacy of the medieval culture of the Indian subcontinent with roots in pre-Buddhist Brahmanism. *Tantra* is a Sanskrit word, meaning the basic warp and weft of threads in weaving. Literally, Tantrism reiterates the Buddhist philosophy of the interwovenness of all things and actions.

Sects and Theology

Unlike democratic monasticism elsewhere, Tibetan monastic orders are highly stratified. Not all monks study religion and theology; many looked after the monastery's administration, farming and business interests. A self-contained community, a Tibetan monastery consists of literally thousands of monks. In the past, one or more sons of a family entered a lifetime of service in the monastery, providing a blessing to his family and a means of sustenance for himself. It is estimated that in the 19th century, one-fifth of Tibet's males were monks.

Tibetan Buddhism is divided into four principal sects whose interpretations and emphasis have developed separately over the centuries, like Catholicism, Protestantism and other orders have in the Christian context.

The oldest Nyingmapa sect is based upon the teachings of Guru Rinpoche. Heavily influenced by Indian Buddhism, the Nyingmapa sect absorbed many tenets of Bon practices and thereby contributed to its popularity and dispersion.

The Kagyudpa order's two principal adherents were the famous translator Marpa and his student, the singer-poet monk Milarepa. The sect is based upon an oral tradition of teaching passed from guru to student. The Sakyapa order dates its birth to 1073 at Sakya Monastery. More rooted in daily life than its more contemplative rivals, it eventually became mired in politics.

The great religious reformer Tsongkhapa is credited with revitalising Buddhism and laying the foundation for the subsequent pre-eminence of his order, the Gelugpa, in 1407. Tsongkhapa reinterpreted the formalistic approach of the earlier Kadampa sect of Reting Monastery, north of Lhasa, that had languished since the mid-11th century when the great teacher Atisha had brought spiritual renewal to Tibet from India. Stressing the purity of Buddhist doctrine, the Gelugpa gradually gained political power, ruling Tibet after the 17th century through its Dalai Lamas.

An ornate silver apron clip

'People of Tibet' by 19th-century painter, H A Oldfield

Today, the Gelugpa is the dominant order but while in the past there have been intense rivalries – including an incident in 1290 when armies of monks from Sakya monastery destroyed rival Drigung monastery – there is no antipathy between the sects now.

Rinpoches and Reincarnation

The designations of the various levels within the Tibetan monastic hierarchy are complex. At the pinnacle is the Dalai Lama (Ocean of Wisdom), a title and concept created by the Mongols to provide spiritual and temporal leaders for Tibet. The first Dalai Lama, a nephew and disciple of Tsongkhapa, was considered a reincarnation of the bodhisattva Chenrezig. Today's 14th incarnation, Tenzin Gyatso, is universally revered by all Tibetan Buddhists and won the Nobel Peace Prize in 1989.

After a Dalai Lama passes from this lifetime, scholars scour the countryside, searching for a boy between the ages of 3 and 5. They look for auspicious signs in his physiognomy and test his ability to recognise objects owned by the previous Dalai Lama. The child is enthroned with great ceremony and until he reaches his majority, a regent rules in his stead.

The Panchen Lama (Great Teacher) originates from another disciple of Tsongkhapa. The first person to hold the office was the teacher of the Fifth Dalai Lama, appointed to head Shigatse's Tashilhunpo Monastery. The 10th Panchen Lama, who was on good terms with the Chinese, died in 1988 and the new one has not yet been found.

Lamas are religious practitioners and teachers. *Rinpoches* (Precious Ones) and *tulkus* (Reincarnate Ones) are lamas who have attained the ultimate spiritual achievement and been recognised as the incarnation of previous lamas. Once identified, the reincarnate child is raised in the monastery and given a religious and secular education by the monks. *Geshes* are monks who have achieved the highest level of knowledge, through study and religious contemplation, in his lifetime.

A small number of Tibetans profess Islam, imported from Central Asia centuries ago. In Lhasa's old quarter you will find a mosque.

Religious Art

Virtually all Tibetan art is associated with the Buddhist faith. Temple layout is based on ancient formulae that dictate the arrangement of rooms, but there can be considerable variation in design and decoration.

Sculpture and painting are similarly reserved for religious subjects. Statues are generally of bronze or copper with highlights in gold and gilt. The few silver statues and plaques (especially at Tashilhunpo) that have survived display a workmanship that attests to a superb eye and a fine hand.

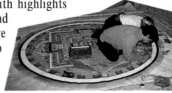

Murals covering the entrance and interior walls of monasteries depict guardian deities and bodhisattvas, and illustrate Buddhist

Creating a mandala

tenets. Some tell the history of Buddhism's growth in Tibet, the life of the Buddha, or, as those at Samye, provide instruction on proper attire and the design of ceremonial utensils. *Thangka* paintings originated as objects of meditation and ritual made transportable for travelling lamas. These *mandalas* and images of Buddhist deities framed in brocade hang from chapel rafters and are either painted or appliqued.

Tibetan literature encompasses myriad Buddhist texts translated from Sanskrit, or commentaries penned by important Tibetan scholars. There are exceptions, however. From the past comes the epic of Gesar of Ling, a legendary monarch who embodies the Tibetan ethos. Milarepa, an ascetic who dwelt in a cave near Nyelam (Nyalam), is best remembered for the beauty of his thousands of songs.

Music and dance are an indispensable extension of prayer and chanting. Masked monks in sumptuous costumes dance at annual ceremonies called *cham* at each monastery, notably during the Ganden Thangka Festival and Lhasa's Yoghurt Festival (Shodun).

A silk-embroidered thangka

Tibetan Life

The Tibetan economy was traditionally based on herding, farming and trading, which in turn typically defined the lifestyles of the people pursuing these livelihoods. As nomadic herdsmen, they tended to eschew permanent houses, preferring to live instead in mobile tents made from woven yak hair. These mobile homes could easily be transported from one grazing region to another. The basis for their existence was the sale of butter made from *dri* (female yak) milk, an integral ingredient in the national drink, salted butter tea. The farmers who gave up the nomadic life built sturdy stone or mud brick houses, cultivating barley, the staple of the Tibetan diet, wheat and a limited variety of vegetables which they consumed, traded or sold in the market.

Before the Chinese Communist government took control of Tibet in 1959, many Tibetans were traders who plied the length of the country, buying and selling goods along commercial routes which extended into China, Nepal and India. With the introduction of Collectivisation by the Communist government in the 1960s, followed by the Cultural Revolution, traditional Tibetan economy was dismantled, lifestyles were uprooted by the commune system, and freedom to move about the country was curtailed. Since the end of the Cultural Revolution in 1976, and with the economic reforms of the late 1970s and early 1980s, the Chinese central government has relaxed some of their controls, allowing rural Tibetans to return to a lifestyle closer to their historic norms.

A merchant class of Tibetans have been allowed to re-emerge in the cities, operating street-side stalls, small businesses, travel agencies and a few guesthouses for foreign travellers. However, these Tibetans are increasingly outnumbered by the Chinese economic immigrants who recently flooded in and who currently control the majority of shops, restaurants and businesses in Tibetan cities and along the main roads. The modern world is rapidly leaving urban Tibetans behind, with many having to settle for low-paying unskilled manual labour jobs, if they can find work.

Another important aspect of Tibetan life was the pursuit of religious studies. Before 1950, as many as one-fifth of the Tibetan male population belonged to a monastery; just the three great Gelugpa monasteries near Lhasa alone had nearly 20,000 monks between them. The monasteries were supported by vast land holdings worked by peasant farmers and herders. In addition, monasteries were also supported by donations from the government and the wealthy noble families. Today, the monasteries that have been allowed to re-open only have a fraction of their former number of monks, though religion still continues to remain as vital and alive as ever in the hearts and minds of the Tibetans.

A pilgrim pauses on the road to salvation

Historical Highlights

AD620–650 Songtsen Gampo, 33rd king of Tibet, rules from the Yarlung Valley. Marries Chinese and Nepalese princesses and moves the capital to Lhasa.

755 Buddhism is established when Trisong Detsen invites two Indian scholars to teach at Samye, build a monastery and train Tibetan monks.

799 The Great Debate of Samye establishes Mahayana Buddhism as the dominant doctrine.

832–842 Bon adherents react against Buddhism and King Langdarma bans the religion.

842 Langdarma is assassinated.

9th–11th century The Tibetan Empire collapses and Buddhism declines. Descendants of the royal family move to West Tibet and start the Guge Kingdom.

Late 11th century 'Second Diffusion' revival of Buddhism begins with invitation of Indian scholar Atisha to Guge.

1249 Mongols establish a 'Patron-Priest' relationship with Sakyas, who rule Tibet for nearly 100 years.

1409 Buddhist reformer Tsongkhapa starts Ganden monastery and establishes the Gelugpa sect.

1578 Sonam Gyatso, the abbot of Drepung, receives the Mongol title of Dalai Lama. Two previous abbots also given the same title, making him the Third Dalai Lama.

1617–82 Reign of the Great Fifth Dalai Lama, who begins construction of the Potala Palace.

1624 Portuguese Jesuit missionaries arrive in Guge.

1728 Manchus assert control.

1788–91 Nepal invades Tibet but is repulsed by Chinese armies.

1855–56 Nepal invades again and secures annual tribute from Tibet.

1904 Younghusband mission occupies Lhasa and gains a treaty.

1911 13th Dalai Lama returns to Tibet as Manchus fall in China leaving Tibet free.

1935 Birth of 14th Dalai Lama.

1950 Communist China invades and occupies eastern Tibet.

1951 Tibet signs 17-Point Agreement with Chinese, granting it domestic autonomy. Communist armies occupy Lhasa.

1959 Insurrection against Chinese rule is quashed; Dalai Lama flees to India.

1965 Tibet becomes an Autonomous Region of China.

Avalokiteshwara masterpiece

1966–76 Cultural Revolution.

1980 First organized group tours allowed in Tibet.

1984 Tibet is opened to independent foreign travellers.

1987 Anti-Chinese demonstrations rock Lhasa.

1989 Riots and martial law stop tourism for 3 months; individual tourists are banned until June 1990.

1990 till present Tibet open to tourists arriving from China and overland from Nepal, with some restrictions on individual travel.

Lhasa and Environs

800 m / 875 yards

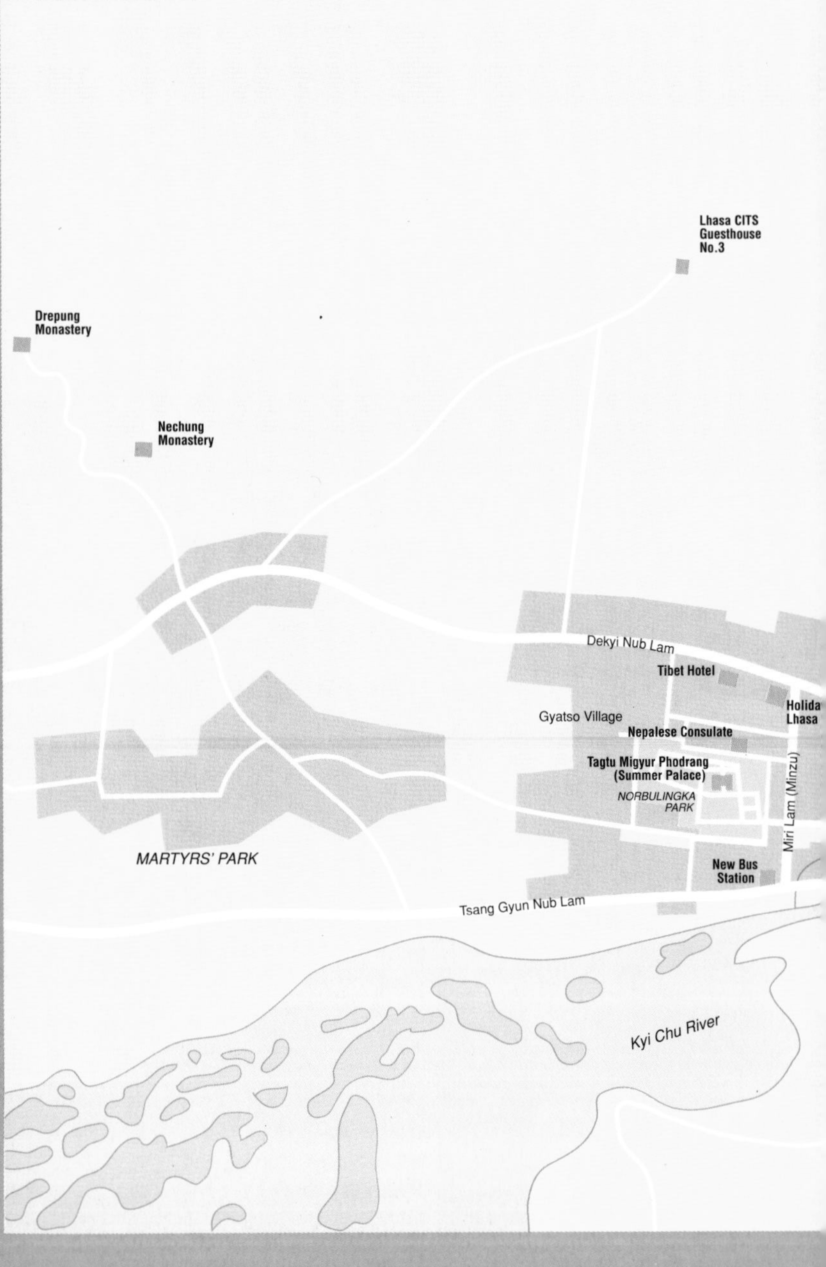

Lhasa CITS
Guesthouse
No.3

Drepung
Monastery

Nechung
Monastery

Dekyi Nub Lam

Tibet Hotel

Gyatso Village

Nepalese Consulate

**Holida
Lhasa**

**Tagtu Migyur Phodrang
(Summer Palace)**

*NORBULINGKA
PARK*

Miri Lam (Minzu)

MARTYRS' PARK

**New Bus
Station**

Tsang Gyun Nub Lam

Kyi Chu River

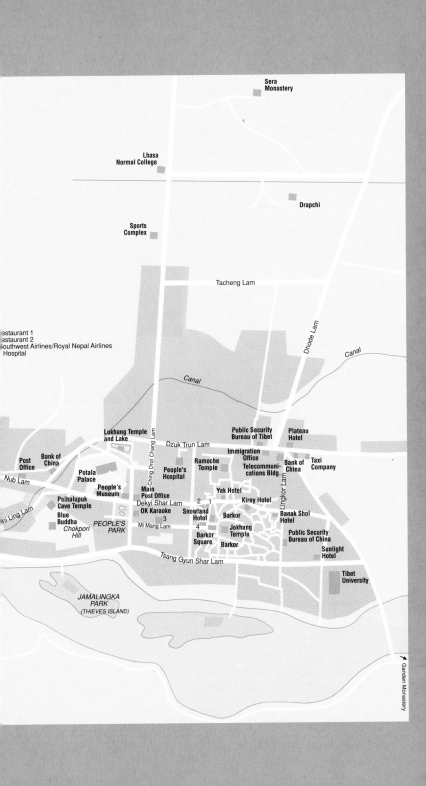

Sera
Monastery

Lhasa
Normal College

Drapchi

Sports
Complex

Tacheng Lam

Dhode Lam

Canal

estaurant 1
estaurant 2
outhwest Airlines/Royal Nepal Airlines
Hospital

Canal

Lukhang Temple
and Lake

Public Security
Bureau of Tibet

Plateau
Hotel

Dzuk Trun Lam

Post
Office

Bank of
China

Immigration
Office

Ramoche
Temple

Telecommuni-
cations Bldg.

Bank of
China

Taxi
Company

Nub Lam

Potala
Palace

People's
Hospital

ni Ling Lam

Palhalupuk
Cave Temple

People's
Museum

Main
Post Office

Yak Hotel

Kirey Hotel

Lingkor Lam

Blue
Buddha

Dekyi Shar Lam

2 1

Chokpori
Hill

OK Karaoke

Snowland
Hotel

Barkor

Banak Shol
Hotel

PEOPLE'S
PARK

3

Mi Mang Lam

4

Barkor
Square

Jokhang
Temple

Public Security
Bureau of China

Barkor

Sunlight
Hotel

Tsang Gyun Shar Lam

Tibet
University

JAMALINGKA
PARK
(THIEVES ISLAND)

Ganden Monastery

Lhasa & Environs

You will find that few journeys begin as dramatically as a flight into the Tibetan capital city of Lhasa. The flight from Chengdu, in southwest China, skirts the northern edge of the towering Himalaya, but even more breathtaking is the 650-km (401-mile), 60-minute flight from Kathmandu that skims less than a thousand metres above the tallest mountains in the world.

Try to sit next to the window on the left side of the plane. Climbing out of the Kathmandu Valley, you fly east along a gleaming wall made up of five of the world's highest mountains. Astride the Nepal-Tibet border is the tallest of them all, the mighty Mount

Fly over alien and unfamiliar terrain

24

Everest at 8,848m (29,028ft), known to the Tibetans as Chomo-lungma and to the Nepalese as Sagarmatha.

The plane banks and like an airborne compass, points north. The green valleys of Nepal and the white peaks of the Himalaya soon drop away and you soar over a mountain desert painted in creams, pinks and pale browns. The surface is faintly etched with hair-like rivers and their dozens of feeders, like capillaries of a gigantic circulatory system, dense black against the buff sands. Treeless, devoid of any greenery, there is no sign of habitation.

Finally, you cross low hills, roughly gouged as if by a woodcarver's adze. Towns appear at the mouths of valleys that narrow as they rise into the mountains. The plane slips closer to earth, gliding onto a lunar landing strip in the middle of desolation. You have arrived at Gongkar (Gonggar) Airport, gateway to Lhasa and some 90km (56 miles) north by road.

Note: Throughout the book, town names are noted first in Tibetan and then if appropriate, in parentheses in Chinese. Religious names are first identified by their Tibetan names (this is after all, Tibet) followed by their original Sanskrit names at the start of each new section. On page 44 is a useful guide on how to identify the key Buddhist images found in temples, and on page 101 a glossary of common Tibetan terms.

1. From Gongkar Airport to Lhasa

Drive past valleys and farms from the airport to Lhasa, stopping by Netang village and monastery. Settle into your hotel, then stroll around People's Park and Gyatso village.

The drive from **Gongkar Airport** to Lhasa introduces you to many of the natural and man-made colours you will encounter during your stay. Valleys are hemmed in by beige mountains which stand in sharp contrast to the blue vault overhead, a sky whose hue verges on cobalt at this high altitude. In the crystalline air, trees are etched against hills and peaks against sky. Occasionally, billowing dust hazes the landscape like the gauze veils called *katas* which Tibetans use to honour gods and each other.

Squat two-storey farm houses dot this moonscape like sand castles on a deserted beach, their mud walls punctuated by small, black-framed trapezoidal windows and topped by tiny turrets. Some embrace courtyards filled with farm animals. Many are whitewashed and defined by ruddy bands just below the roofline. From the turrets fly the colours humans have imposed on the landscape; the five-colour flags symbolise sky (blue), clouds (white), fire (red), water (green) and earth (yellow).

The road soon parallels and then crosses the **Yarlung Tsangpo river**, which flows 2,900km (1,800 miles) from west to east across the Tibetan plateau before it loops south to enter Bangladesh. The

Buddha rock carving on the road to Lhasa

Yarlung Valley is the birthplace of the Tibetan civilization.

At the base of the Chuwori (Chaksamchari) peak, the road turns right to cross the Yarlung Tsangpo river and right again along the banks of its feeder, the Kyi Chu river, as you begin the ascent into Lhasa's valley.

On the left, 20km (12 miles) before reaching Lhasa, is **Netang Monastery** with its famed **Drolma Lhakhang** (open daily 9.30am–6pm) dedicated to Drolma (Tara) and typical in layout of many you will see on your journey through Tibet. Netang is one of the most important and well-preserved monasteries in Tibet.

The 11th-century Drolma Lhakhang (*lhakhang* meaning chapel or inner sanctuary) was founded by Atisha (Jowo Je), the celebrated Indian Buddhist monk who was instrumental in reviving Buddhism in the mid-11th century. Its first chapel contains a victory *stupa* symbolising the present Sakyamuni Buddha's triumph over temptation in his quest for enlightenment. Look for the statue of Atisha meditating, flanked by the Eight Medicine Buddhas.

The middle temple is dedicated to Drol-Jang (Green Tara), patron goddess of Tibet. To the right of the principal Buddha image sits Drolma, the largest of 21 images of her in the room. Until they were returned to Bengal in the 1960s, Atisha's ashes were kept in an urn on the left side of the altar.

A mound in the middle of the third chapel is all that remains of a throne on which Atisha sat to instruct new monks in the tenets of Buddhism. Before it is another image of him wearing the red pointed hat which identifies his statues. On leaving the monastery, spin the prayer wheels for an auspicious start to your journey towards Lhasa on the far horizon.

Your first day in **Lhasa** (3,650m/11,970ft) should be spent quietly, allowing your body time to acclimatise. Drink as much liquids as you can, read, or take a stroll. If you find that the altitude does not bother you, venture further afield but walk slowly, and be sure not to exert yourself. Several sites give you the flavour of the city. The **Barkor Square** and Barkor **market** and pilgrimage route around the **Jokhang** temple is the Tibetan heart of Lhasa (*see page 34*). Downtown and facing the **Potala Palace** in the Chinese part of town is a man-made lake and on its bank is **People's Park**, offering a superb view of the Potala towering above you. Sit on a park bench to watch Tibetans relaxing or have your photo taken on a shaggy pony against a Potala backdrop. In the middle of the lake is a pagoda whose upper storey commands a panoramic view of the surrounding area.

If you feel up to it, spend the late afternoon walking around **Gyatso village** just behind the Holiday Inn Lhasa Hotel. Walk west on Dekyi Nub Lam Road, turning just past the Tibet Hotel into a narrow lane that takes you into the heart of this typical Lhasa village. Look at the houses and the yak horns set over the door frames for protection. When night falls, return to your hotel for dinner.

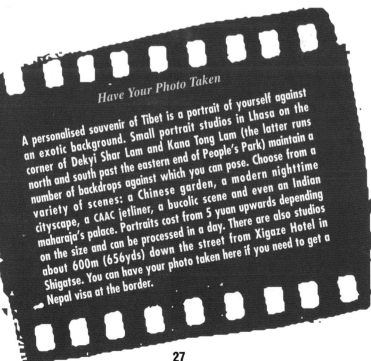

Have Your Photo Taken

A personalised souvenir of Tibet is a portrait of yourself against an exotic background. Small portrait studios in Lhasa on the corner of Dekyi Shar Lam and Kana Tong Lam (the latter runs north and south past the eastern end of People's Park) maintain a number of backdrops against which you can pose. Choose from a variety of scenes: a Chinese garden, a modern nighttime cityscape, a CAAC jetliner, a bucolic scene and even an Indian maharaja's palace. Portraits cost from 5 yuan upwards depending on the size and can be processed in a day. There are also studios about 600m (656yds) down the street from Xigaze Hotel in Shigatse. You can have your photo taken here if you need to get a Nepal visa at the border.

2. Potala Palace and Norbulingka

Begin with a visit to the most enduring symbol of Tibet – the Potala Palace. After lunch, proceed to Norbulingka, also known as the Jewel Park, the summer residence of the Dalai Lama.

While other Tibetan monuments are more important in religious terms, the **Potala Palace** (Monday to Saturday 9am–noon) is the most enduring symbol of Tibet. The most complex monument ever built in Tibet, the edifice rises over 117m (383ft) high and is reputed to house some 10,000 shrines and over 200,000 images. The Potala is undergoing major renovations but check with your travel agent as conditions change from time to time. Remember to always walk in a clockwise direction around the shrines and sacred images and statues, or you risk offending the monks and pilgrims.

In the 7th century, King Songtsen Gampo built a modest palace atop the Red Hill, on the present site of the Potala. Although the original structure was burned by Chinese invaders shortly after his death, two rooms have survived.

The Potala, whose 13 storeys house a thousand rooms, dates from 1645, when the Fifth Dalai Lama first began erecting a palace that would serve as a sacred and administrative centre. It was also the seat of government and before the mid-18th century served as a fortress. Work on the lower section, called the White Palace, was completed in 1648. The Fifth Dalai Lama died in 1682, 12 years before the building's finial, the Red Palace, was finished. To ensure it was completed without delay, the Regent, Desi Sangye Gyatso, concealed the Great Fifth's death, informing the world that the leader had retired into a life of religious contemplation.

The Potala served succeeding Dalai Lamas until 1959. One of Tibet's most impressive and enduring monuments, it was protected by the Chinese Army from Red Guards during the Cultural Revolution on orders, it is said, from Chinese premier Zhou En Lai himself. As a result, many of its chapels and treasures are intact, virtually unchanged since the 17th century.

The Potala's dim hallways evoke the surreal mysticism associated with Tibetan Buddhism. Rough-clad pilgrims press into narrow chapels, spooning yak butter from glass jars into silver and gold lamps. Flames made eternal by faith illuminate the Buddha images and the awed, devout faces that gaze up at them.

Tourists groups are driven up

The Potala Palace in the clouds

A gold encrusted wooden door at the Potala

the western flank of the hill to the back door, thus saving them the long climb up the slope; pilgrims enter from the main gate above Dekyi Shar Lam.

Enter the great doors to the long, narrow **Tungri Lhakhang** of the **Red Palace**. Here are found many of the deities you will encounter on your journey through Tibet, so take the opportunity to study them. At the centre is an image of the Potala's creator, the Great Fifth Dalai Lama, seated next to the Sakyamuni Buddha. Before him are manifestations of Guru Rinpoche (Padmasambhava).

To the left of the Great Fifth is the Bodhisattva of Compassion, Chenrezig (Avalokiteshwara), King Songtsen Gampo and a disciple of Atisha, the famous lama Dromton who founded the Kadampa monastery at Reting. Next come images of the First through Fourth Dalai Lamas; on the far left is a *stupa* with relics of the 11th Dalai Lama. An identifying label has been affixed to the base of each image. Study these labels well because the Potala is the last monastery where you will be given such help.

In front of the Tungri Lhakhang is the **Assembly Hall**, used by every Dalai Lama since the Great Fifth. Murals on the front and back walls depict the Buddha Sakyamuni's life.

The **Fifth Dalai Lama Lhakhang** holds the enormous golden tomb of its namesake, the largest in the Potala. To the left and right are the reliquary stupas of the 12th and 10th Dalai Lamas.

Opposite the Tungri Lhakhang is the **Rigzin Lhakhang**, honouring eight Indian Tantric teachers led by Guru Rinpoche, who appears in eight different manifestations. The **Lamrim Lhakhang** holds a statue of the great reformer Tsongkhapa made in Qinghai province, and 70 images of famous Gelugpa lamas.

Climb the stairs to the next floor. The chapels around the courtyard are closed to the public, but take a moment to observe the

Lighted butter lamps at Potala chapel

murals depicting festivities during the Monlam Chenmo (Great Prayer Festival) and the construction of the Potala. Climb to the next floor. The **meditation cave of King Songtsen Gampo** is one of two rooms of his palace which survived a disastrous fire. Directly in front of the door is a statue of the king with his military minister Lampugawa and another minister, Tomni Sambhota, who was sent to India to learn Sanskrit and to find a script suitable for written Tibetan. On Songtsen Gampo's left are his Nepalese and Chinese queens. It is said the ladies were later incarnated and revered as the Drolma Jang (Green Tara) and Drolma Karpo (White Tara) respectively.

Situated in the **Tsepame Lhakhang**, dominated by the throne of the Eighth Dalai Lama, are two Drolma images and nine images of Tsepame (Amitayus). The Buddha Sakyamuni and the Eight Bodhisattvas are the principal images in the **Sakyamuni Lhakhang**.

One of the most important rooms in the Potala is the **Dukor Lhakhang**, Wheel of Time, dedicated to the Dukor (Kalachakra) and the *lamas* who have passed its complex Tantric practice down through the generations. Its masterpiece is a very large, and superb representation of the intricate *mandala* rendered in copper and gold. Climb the stairs to the top floor.

The **Lokeshwara Lhakhang** is the only other room of Songtsen Gampo's original palace that escaped the fire. It is regarded as the most sacred room in the Potala; note how the pilgrims prostrate reverently

Guardian snow lions

to touch objects embedded in the floor to obtain blessings.

The temple's central image is Chenrezig, said to have come from India during Songtsen Gampo's reign. To the right is the fierce guardian, Chana Dorje (Vajrapani) and beyond are statues of the Eighth, Ninth and Tenth Dalai Lamas. On the left is an image of Tsongkhapa.

The chapels containing tombs of the Seventh, Eighth, and Ninth Dalai Lamas are closed to the public.

The impressive golden stupa of the **13th Dalai Lama's Tomb** is so high it extends into the upper floor. The murals on either side of the door depict the 13th Dalai Lama with other important personages from his life. He died mysteriously on the road to China, and the **Sixth Dalai Lama's Lhakhang** contains his throne. He is the only one of the 13 Dalai Lamas without a tomb.

The gold, thousand-armed Chenrezig is the dominant image in the **Vijaya Lhakhang**. The **Mandala Lhakhang** was built by the Seventh Dalai Lama and contains three superb three-dimensional Tantric *mandalas*, numerous Drolmas and some fine murals.

A Potala pilgrim

The **Jampa Lhakhang** is dominated by a large and finely-crafted statue of the Jampa (Maitreya), Buddha of the Future. To his left is the image of Lhasa's guardian deity, Palden Lhamo (Sridevi), whose face is so terrifying that she is veiled. Behind her are 1,000 Tsepame Buddhas. On the left, next to the altar with the photograph of the present 14th Dalai Lama, is Drolma and a victory *stupa* and to the right is the Dukor. On the left are important *Tengyur* scriptures, said to have been written by Tsongkhapa himself.

Descend three floors to the **inner courtyard** where masked monks often dance during the religious festivals. In the far left-hand corner is a public toilet.

Exit the courtyard to the terrace. Walk to the parapet to gaze down on Lhasa and then head to the left into the **White Palace** and the chambers of the 13th and 14th Dalai Lamas. The first room is the **Audience Hall**, used by both Dalai Lamas whose portraits are to the left and right of the throne. The mural on the back wall depicts the life of the Buddha. The room to the left was the **library** of both leaders. In the **meditation room** you will see many miniature statues.

The remaining rooms of the White Palace are administrative offices and storerooms, and are closed to the public. Descend the broad flights of stairs that zigzag across the face of the Potala.

Return to your hotel for lunch and in the afternoon, proceed to the **Norbulingka,** Jewel Park (open daily 10am–1pm, 3.30–6pm). The Norbulingka was designated as a summer retreat by the Seventh Dalai Lama in 1755, but most of the buildings were not erected

The summer palace of Norbulingka attracts both tourists and pilgrims

until the reigns of the 13th and 14th Dalai Lamas. Each spring, as the chill air warmed and the willow trees began to blossom, the Dalai Lama would leave the Potala in a grand procession to the Norbulingka – a large complex of palaces, chapels pavilions and gardens – where he would spend the next 6 months. The 14th Dalai Lama was living here in 1959 when the Chinese Army began shelling Lhasa. Together with his retinue, the Dalai Lama left quietly during the night for the Indian border and exile. The Norbulingka was shelled the day after, and during the Cultural Revolution, even further damage was inflicted.

The large and rustic 4sq km (2sq mile) park surrounding the complex is quite beautiful. Through the elaborate gate guarded by ornate silver snow lions, you pass the first of many gardens and encounter the **Kelsang Phodrang** (palace) of the Eighth Dalai Lama. The audience hall contains some very fine *thangkas* depicting the Drolma Karpo.

Further on is an artificial lake dating from the Eighth Dalai Lama's reign. The pavilion holds some non-religious painted panels and most likely served as a place to relax and talk. Turn right just beyond it to the **Drunzig Palace** which houses the library.

Beyond the lake is the showpiece of the park, the magnificent **Tagtu Migyur Phodrang** or Summer Palace. Completed in 1956 for His Holiness, the handsome building is ornately decorated with Tibetan carvings and paintings. Inside, the melange of European trinkets and Tibetan artefacts reflect the enquiring personality of the 14th Dalai Lama and his interest in the West. Climb the stairs to the **Audience Hall** on the second floor. Silver images of Dorje Chang (Vajradhara), Jampa and Jambeyang (Manjushri) stand on the altar while above them a finely-woven brocade banner depicts the major Indian Buddhist philosophers. Above the Dalai Lama's throne along the right wall is a *thangka* portraying Dorje Jigche (Yamantaka).

The most intriguing aspect of the hall is its murals. Painted in fine detail like an Indian Moghul miniature, the murals on the left wall trace the history of Tibet. The story begins with the Buddha's concern that Tibet had no people, leading Chenrezig to turn himself into a monkey and descend to the mountain realm to produce offspring (*see page 10*). The murals on the left part of the front wall relate the history of Samye monastery, and on the right that of Ganden, Drepung, Sera and Tashilhunpo monasteries. Portrayed to the right of His Holiness's throne are the lives of the 1st to 14th Dalai Lamas. On the same floor is the 14th Dalai Lama's **study**. One wall is covered with a beautifully embroidered *thangka* of Atisha (Jowo Je), a gift from Bangladesh. On the opposite wall is an old Russian radio.

Next is the **bedroom** with its huge 1956 Phillips radio, a gift from India. Passing the bathroom, you enter the **reception hall**. The room is dominated by the Dalai Lama's throne, rendered in orange-gold, and opposite are images of Atisha, Jampa and Tsongkhapa. The most interesting parts of the room, however, are its photograph-like murals, portraying Tibetan notables.

Painted by Amdo Jampa, who recently returned from exile in India, they detail the history of Tsongkhapa, Sakyamuni and the present Dalai Lama with regents and tutors above him and on the left, ministers and relatives. His mother is on the right. Depicted in their native costumes at the bottom right are tribes from the different parts of Tibet. On the lower left are portraits of foreign dignitaries including ambassadors, British resident Hugh Richardson, and Kawaguchi Ekai, the Japanese who disguised himself as a monk and resided in Tibet from 1900 to 1903. This ends the tour.

The reception desk offers several interesting books, including a voluminous treatise on Tibetan medicine, a highly developed combination of indigenous, Chinese herbal and ayurvedic medicine practices of the lamas.

Farther west in the extensive Norbulingka grounds is a zoo which houses a number of endangered Tibetan animals, with living conditions that are less than ideal.

Return to your hotel for dinner, or try any one of the restaurants recommended on page 85.

Image of Guru Rinpoche

3. Jokhang and Ramoche Temples

Begin your tour at the end of Barkor Square at the holy Jokhang temple. Lunch at Barkor Cafe before visiting the 7th-century Ramoche temple. Dine on Tibetan cuisine, then croon to your heart's content at a karaoke bar.

Today, you become a pilgrim to the holiest temple in Tibet. After breakfast, proceed to the broad **Barkor Square**, at whose eastern end is the **Jokhang** (open daily 10am–1.30pm), which shelters the Jowo Sakyamuni, Tibet's most revered image. As you approach its great doors you will encounter a crowd of Tibetans crossing your path from right to left as they perambulate clockwise around the Jokhang. Join the procession.

The **Barkor** refers to the middle of the three concentric holy circuits around the Jokhang Temple. The Barkor circles the circumference of Jokhang itself and is the most popular. The most important, the outermost **Lingkor** (*see page 45*), takes pilgrims around the principal religious landmarks of the city. The third and innermost circle, the **Nangkor**, is within the precincts of the Jokhang.

The Barkor circuit runs through the heart of the old city where life has changed little over the centuries. About one quarter the way around is the **Mani Lhakhang**, rebuilt in 1987 and sheltering an enormous prayer wheel. The circuit brings you back to the Jokhang's broad front doors. To enter, thread your way gingerly past pilgrims prostrating themselves full length.

The Jokhang was the first religious building erected by King Songtsen Gampo when he moved his capital to Lhasa in the 7th century. Legend says that the site was originally a lake inhabited by demons and had to be filled in before construction could begin. A sacred goat carried stones to provide a solid foundation.

The Jokhang was built to hold the Buddha image brought to Tibet by Songtsen Gampo's Nepalese Queen Bhrikuti; the nearby Ramoche Temple was built to house the image donated by the Chinese Queen Wencheng. After her husband's death, Wencheng is said to have switched the two images, placing hers in the more impressive Jokhang.

In the centre of the main hall is the thousand-armed Chenrezig (Avalokiteshvara) and to the left and right are images of Guru

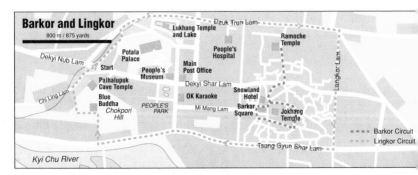

Barkor Square – the social centre of Lhasa

Rinpoche (Padmasambhava) and Jampa (Maitreya) Buddha.

The Jokhang's principal attractions lie in its many chapels. The one in the left corner at the far end of the hall holds a statue of Tsongkhapa, commissioned by the great reformer himself, who is said to have been astonished by its likeness.

The chapel to the right holds Opame (Amitabha), the Buddha of Infinite Light. Pilgrims make offerings here, asking to be purified so that they can enter the Jowo chapel without tainted souls.

The central chapel holds the Jowo Sakyamuni, the most important image in Tibet. It is an impressive statue with a magnificent crown of gold, coral and turquoise. Pilgrims often touch their heads against the image in adoration. Above it stands a bronze garuda clasping two *nagas* (serpents). Behind the Jowo Sakyamuni are the head and shoulders of an older Buddha image, said to have occupied the chamber before the Jowo's arrival and who, according to tradition, now regards himself as the Jowo's guardian. Note the beautifully carved wooden ceiling.

The fourth chapel along the right-hand wall holds a fine statue of Jampa which monks carry in procession around the Barkor during the Monlam Chenmo (Great Prayer) festival (*see page 86*). In the right-hand corner along the wall nearest the entrance doors, the **Chapel of the Dharma Kings** contains images that somehow escaped destruction. The three most important statues are of Songtsen Gampo, Trisong Detsen and Repachen.

Most interesting are the murals along the wall by the door to this chapel. On the left is a fine portrait of the Potala depicting a festival in ancient times. The right-hand mural portrays the construction of the Jokhang. See the sacred goat hauling stones from the lake while Princess Wencheng tosses her ring into it to ensure that the lake will not overflow again.

Monks gathered outside the Jokhang

Climb to the second floor. Set in the centre along the front wall, the **Chapel of Songtsen Gampo** is dedicated to the founder of the Jokhang. It holds a statue of him with his wives Bhrikuti and Wencheng. The Seven Heroic Buddhas, Tsongkhapa and his two main disciples are arranged around him and in front of Songtsen Gampo rests a silver pitcher from which the monarch was said to have sipped *chang* (barley beer). Prior to 1959, the pitcher was carried in an annual procession to the houses of Lhasa nobles who would be served cups of *chang* to honour them. If the monks permit you, climb to the roof for a superb view of the Potala.

As you exit the Jokhang to Barkor Square, peer through the two enclosures holding three inscribed steles. Written in Chinese in the two semi-circles are the ancient cures for smallpox. The slender stele rising above the walls records a Sino-Tibetan treaty of AD821 stipulating, ironically, that Tibet enjoys equal status with China and sovereignty over its territory, and that its borders are inviolate; the penalty for crossing them without permission is immediate arrest and expulsion.

Lunch at the **Barkor Cafe** on the southwest end of Barkor Square. Managed by the Holiday Inn Lhasa Hotel, the cafe offers snacks and tea. Sit with friends on the balcony, enjoy the sunshine and watch the world go by.

North of the Barkor on Je Bum Gang Lam (walk behind the Jokhang and turn left, crossing Dekyi Shar Lam) is **Ramoche** (open daily 10am–1pm, 3.30–6pm), a small but important temple, contemporaneous with the Jokhang.

Four tall brass prayer wheels stand sentinel at the bold red entrance gate set with lotus-shaped discs and long reinforcing straps made of iron. The huge girth of the columns supporting the gate roof suggest the size of the trees that once grew in Tibet.

The main hall is unremarkable aside from its newness so proceed to the main shrine at the far end. Four Guardian Deities protect the short flight of steps to the image of Mikyopa (Akshobhya Vajra), said to show the young Sakyamuni Buddha at the age of eight. Now restored, the image displays superb workmanship. Ask to climb to the roof for a good view of the neighbourhood before returning to Barkor Square.

For a Tibetan dinner, head for the **Gang Gyen Sakang** at Dekyi Shar Lam. It serves an array of Tibetan dishes that allows you to sample a variety of flavours. The setting is worth the price; a dimly-lit room filled with raucous Tibetans enjoying themselves.

After dinner, drop in at the **OK Karaoke Bar** on Kana Tong Lam near the eastern entrance to People's Park for a bottle of Lhasa beer and an evening of singing.

4. Great Monasteries: Drepung, Nechung and Sera

A visit to Drepung Monastery, once Tibet's largest monastery, then on to Nechung Monastery, the residence of Tibet's State Oracle. Continue to the peaceful and charming Sera Monastery.

After breakfast at your hotel, drive 8km (5 miles) west of Lhasa to **Drepung Monastery** (open daily 10am–1pm), standing in the shadow of a tall mountain.

Founded in 1416 by one of Tsongkhapa's two most important disciples, Jamyan Choje Tashi Palden (his other disciple founded Sera), Drepung became an important Gelugpa religious centre. It also served as the residence of the Third, Fourth and Fifth Dalai Lamas until the latter built the Potala Palace. Drepung means 'Heap of Rice' and the fertility of its fields and gardens supported a monastic community that before 1959 ranked as Tibet's largest with 7,770 monks; today, there are only about 450 left.

Although the Chinese billeted soldiers here, Drepung suffered only minor damage during the Cultural Revolution. Start at the **Ganden Phodrang**, climbing two flights of stairs to the upper courtyard. Here, monks perform the masked dance during the an-

The wheel of life

nual Yoghurt festival (*see page 88*) while Drepung's gigantic 35m by 50m (38yds by 55yds) *thangka* is displayed on the wall. Across the courtyard is a nondescript assembly hall. At the far end is a chapel containing a fine image of the Fifth Dalai Lama. Behind it is Dorje Jigche (Yamantaka) and behind him, Jambeyang (Manjushri).

Climb the right or left-hand stairway – the middle one is reserved for the Dalai Lama – turning left at the terrace and proceeding through the low door on the left. This small audience chamber is dominated by a large throne used by the 14th Dalai Lama; the atmosphere provided by skylights through which sunlight streams in and sets the murals and *thangkas* aglow. Along the walls are shelves holding sacred manuscripts under which pilgrims prostrate themselves, receiving by osmosis the wisdom of ancient scholars.

Exit the Ganden Phodrang and climb the hill to the **Assembly Hall**. Before entering, pause to look at the superbly restored murals of the four Guardian Deities and other figures. The biggest assembly hall in Tibet, the enormous room could hold all of Drepung's 7,770 monks at one time; the sight and sound of a chanting session must have been overwhelming. With the number of Drepung's monks greatly reduced, it is too cavernous to be of practical use so the monks use the Loseling College down the hill.

The first two chapels on the left hold the tombs of the Fourth and Third Dalai Lamas but are closed to the public. Arranged along the back wall of the Assembly Hall are key deities and personalities of Tibetan Buddhism. The long cabinet on the right wall holds Drepung's huge *thangka*.

The chapel behind the altar is dominated by the Pankara, Sakyamuni and Jampa buddhas –

Drepung monks survey the Lhasa Valley

the Buddhas of the Past, Present and Future. Behind the trio are nine replicas of the Dukor (Kalachakra). Eight huge Bodhisattvas stand along the side walls to the right, and to the left of the entrance door are the fierce guardians, Tamdin (Hayagriva) and Chana Dorje (Vajrapani).

Exit the hall and climb to the next floor. At the back is a chapel filled with several beautifully wrought images. Central among them is the head and shoulders of Jampa (Maitreya) Buddha, the rest of whose body is in a closed chapel in the floor below. A number of lovely images are found in front of it.

The **Drolma Lhakhang** to the right holds three images of the Guardian Deity but its prize collection is the 114-volume set of the *Kangyur*, the sacred discourses of the Buddha. Prepared under

the tutelage of the Fifth Dalai Lama himself, the scriptures are written in gilt ink and bound in fragrant sandalwood decorated with ivory.

Climb one more storey to the roof. The room on the left contains statues of all the kings and Dalai Lamas of Tibet. Two other chapels are dedicated to Jampa and Sakyamuni. Enjoy the view.

Descend to the entrance and exit into the courtyard. Walk to the right and up the hill. Before reaching the Ngagpa College – which holds little of interest – turn right onto a path leading to the **Jambeyang Temple** set directly behind the main assembly hall you have just visited. It holds an impressive image of Jambeyang (Manjushri) carved onto a large stone.

Continue around the outside of the Assembly Hall, descending the path and the stairway to **Loseling College**. Like those in Loseling's chapels, the statues in the assembly hall here honour lamas and rinpoches (*see page 19*) associated with the college and the monastery. As you leave the eastern doorway of the college, peek into the kitchen opposite with its array of wooden utensils banded with brass and copper.

A 5-minute walk brings you to **Nechung Monastery** (open daily 9am–12pm, 2.30–4pm), the residence of Tibet's State Oracle without whose advice no Tibetan government would make a major decision. Early photos show him at his annual ceremony to the Meru Nyinba shrine behind the Jokhang, staggering beneath the weight of an impossibly heavy costume. Entering a trance, he sought to convey the thoughts of Dorje Drakden, a deity believed to be the special protector of Tibetan rulers. After 1959, the Oracle left Tibet and now serves the Dalai Lama at Dharmasala, India.

Recognising the Oracle's significance, the Chinese almost destroyed Nechung Monastery during the Cultural Revolution. It has

A restored wall mural at Nechung Monastery

Tea time at Nechung monastery

been restored but only 12 monks live at the monastery today.

Enter the doors with paintings of withered human bodies to reach a temple on the left dedicated to Dorje Drakden; an aged *thangka* depicts him as a wise old sage. Two images of him stand on either side of a tree stump said to have been inhabited by the deity. A second chapel holds a Sakyamuni image and three lovely *thangkas* depicting Ekajati, Dorje Jigche and Tsedrekma.

Leave the monastery, turn right and climb the stairs to two chapels on the upper floor. The first served as an audience hall for the Fifth Dalai Lama and holds a fine representation of him. Look also at the well-crafted *thangka* of Demchok (Chakrasamvara). The second chapel is dedicated to Tsongkhapa.

As evidence of the fine workmanship of modern artists, climb to the rooftop chapel holding a superb statue of Guru Rinpoche (Padmasambhava), crafted by a Tibetan sculptor in 1981. Return to your hotel for a leisurely lunch.

After lunch, proceed to the great **Sera Monastery** (open daily 10am–4pm), 5km (3 miles) north of Lhasa. Sera's setting is one of Lhasa's prettiest. Like Drepung, it hugs the ridge that forms the northern wall of the Kyi Chu Valley, but it is the trees and bucolic atmosphere that make it so charming.

Like Drepung and Ganden monasteries (*see page 42*), Sera reigned as an important Gelugpa centre of learning. Once a community of more than 5,000 monks, it was virtually extinguished by the Chinese. The restored monastery sits below the brow of a hill on which Tsongkhapa built a hermitage and spent several years meditating. One of the monks' disciples began building Sera in 1419, completing it a few years later.

Sera's fame comes in part from the active role it has played in Tibetan politics. While Drepung concentrated on Tantric religious studies, Sera's politicised monks became embroiled in national affairs, culminating in a foiled plot to kill the Regent in 1947 .

Little about Sera's peaceful setting would suggest such a tumultuous history. At the top of a long dusty road hemmed in by rock walls and willow trees is the **Tsokchen Assembly Hall**. The largest building in Sera, its cavernous interior is decorated with superb silk *thangkas*. The principal image in the hall is that of Sera's founder, Jamchen Choje, but more remarkable is a beautiful seated Jampa which rises 9m (30ft), so high that the head extends into the second storey.

As you enter the upper floor, examine the fine statue of Chenrezig (Avalokiteshvara) on the far left. Continue into the main hall to look at the top of the Jampa statue that protrudes from the floor be-

The yellow hats of Drepung

low. Fine workmanship and attention to detail make it one of Sera's most striking images.

Leave Tsokchen Assembly Hall. If you are feeling energetic, climb the hill to a replica of Tsongkhapa's retreat. Along the way are lovely bas relief stone carvings of Drolma (Tara), Tsongkhapa and others. To the west is the **Debating Garden**, a tranquil spot where monks gather to discuss the finer points of doctrine learned during the morning studies. There are few more pleasant settings in which to witness the graceful and distinctive hand and body movement which are an integral part of the discourse. Monks debate here from 3–5pm each day except Sunday .

Beyond the garden is the **Sera Je College**, the most interesting of Sera's buildings. Its main hall with 108 (an auspicious number in Buddhism) pillars holds images of luminaries associated with Sera itself. The murals are new, and on the left wall they depict the life story of the Buddha.

The first chapel leads to the **Tamdin Chapel** which attracts pilgrims from around Tibet. Legend says that Tsongkhapa himself found the Tamdin (Hayagriva) image and had the chapel built around it. Note the old battle weapons hanging on the walls.

Beyond the altar are chapels dedicated to Jampa, Tsongkhapa and a smiling Jambeyang. Legend suggests that the latter tilts towards the window, the better to hear the theological debates in the garden below. Upstairs, in another chapel dedicated to Tamdin, are fine statues of Guardian Deities.

Just west of Sera is **Sera Ngagpa College**. Sera's oldest building, this Tantric college is supported by columns and capitals displaying superb carvings and paintings. Inside is a temple domi-

Golden roofs of Sera Monastery

nated by Sakyamuni backed by a beautifully carved wooden screen.

Walk downhill to **Sera Me College**. Sera Me's main hall holds a Sakyamuni image with a finely crafted halo. Five chapels surround the hall. The first is dedicated to Taog Chogyal, protector of the East. Sera is regarded as the creator of the Tibetan Buddhist concept of the *vajra* or *dorje* (symbolic thunderbolt), originally a Hindu icon but adapted by Tibetans to signify the power of enlightenment. A number of these, cased in bronze, hang from a beam.

The second chapel is dedicated to Tsongkhapa, the third to the Buddhas of the Three Ages, and the fourth holds the Miwang Jowo, commissioned in the 15th century by an influential Lhasa family. The final chapel is also dedicated to Tsongkhapa.

Return to your hotel. You will have sufficient time before dinner to take one of the shorter itineraries described on pages 45–47.

For a culinary change, visit one of the Tibetan or Chinese restaurants on Dekyi Nub Lam near the Holiday Inn Lhasa Hotel. Few proprietors speak English so select by pointing to whatever looks interesting on other diners' tables.

5. Ganden Monastery

Travel east of Lhasa to explore one of the biggest and most important Gelugpa monasteries in Tibet.

A daily bus runs to **Ganden Monastery** (open daily 9.30am–6pm), 40km (25 miles) east of Lhasa, leaving from the southeastern corner of the Barkor at 6.30am. Hiring a landcruiser from a local travel company enables you to spend more time exploring the ruins. Note that women are not permitted in some of the chapels.

After years of wandering from monastery to monastery across Central Tibet, Tsongkhapa, founder of the Gelugpa order, decided to build his own monastery at Mount Drokri. By 1417, 70 buildings had been completed but he lived only two more years.

Ganden soon became renowned as one of the biggest and most important Gelugpa monasteries in Tibet. In 1959, more than 5,000 monks lived and studied here but were dispersed soon after the Tibetan agitation for independency was quashed. By the onset

Ganden: antique city, modern ruins

of the Cultural Revolution, Ganden was deserted, but the Red Guards, recognising its symbolic importance, destroyed it by bombing and shelling, setting explosives amidst the ancient structures and finally dismantling it brick by brick in a fury of mindless destruction perhaps unparalleled in history. Today, many of the buildings remain in ruins.

From the entrance, walk uphill to the first building of substance, **Tsongkhapa's Tomb**, which is found where the path curves left. The most imposing building on the hill, the red-walled shrine contains a wide courtyard that leads to a protector chapel holding a copper and gold statue of Sakyamuni. Climb the staircase to the tomb itself. Legend says that when Tsongkhapa died, he transformed his body into that of a 16-year-old boy. The huge gold and silver stupa encasing it was broken by Red Guards who were shocked to find the undecomposed body in perfect condition. Today, only fragments of the *stupa* remain.

Continue along the left path to the **Amdo Khangtsen** which once housed monks from Amdo, Tsongkhapa's birthplace in the northeast of Tibet. Its main chapel is decorated with lovely brocade banners and painted murals. Look along the floor for a small glass case holding what is claimed to be the eye of the Dharmaraja Guardian Deity.

The next building, the Dreu Khangtsen, holds little of interest but the path leads to a ridge which affords a superb view of the surrounding area. Continue on the pilgrimage path around the back of the ridge to reach the **Throne Holder's Residence**. Alternatively, you can get to it by retracing your steps to the intersection just above Tsongkhapa's Tomb and turning left.

The Throne Holder's Residence was the home of the Ganden Tripa, the abbot of Ganden. The upper chapel holds statues of Tsongkhapa and his two main disciples, flanked by a set of the *Kangyur*, sacred discourses of the Buddha, and the Ganden Tripa's throne.

Next is the **Dzom Chen Khang**, whose throne contains the jacket of Tsongkhapa. Adjacent to it is the room where Tsongkhapa died; its walls painted with murals depicting deities.

If you are drawn to the mystery of ruins, you can wander at will among the ghosts of the past, watching the sun set over the complex and returning to Lhasa late in the evening.

Identifying Buddhist Images

Atisha (also Jowo Je): The Indian master and teacher who helped revive Tibetan Buddhism in the 11th century. Monk's robe, red-pointed hat with long ear flaps, seated in lotus position with hands before chest in teaching position.

Chana Dorje (Vajrapani): The Bodhisattva of energy and power appears in benevolent or ferocious aspect. Dark blue body, *dorje* in extended right hand, tiger skin wrapped around his waist and a snake around his neck.

Chenrezig (Avalokiteshwara): The four-armed Boddhisattva of Compassion and Protector of Tibet. Seated in lotus position, white body, right hand holds a lotus flower, left hand prayer beads, central two arms clasped at the chest.

Demchok (Chakrasamvara): The Circle of Bliss is a wrathful multi-armed deity that resembles Dukor. Has four faces, and each hand holds a ritual object, including a long staff. Neither leg of his consort touches the ground.

Dorje Jigche (Yamantaka): Lord of Death, manifestation of the Hindu Shiva and guardian of the Gelugpa sect. Dark blue, squat, 34 arms, 16 legs, 9 heads, the main head that of a buffalo, necklace of heads, holds a skull cup and knife.

Drol-jang (or Drolma Jang, the Green Tara): The motherly aspect of compassion, regarded as Tibet's patron saint. Green body, seated on a lotus throne, right leg extended, left hand holding stem of a lotus flower.

Drol-kar (or Drolma Karpo, the White Tara): The seven-eyed Drolma, with eyes on the face, one on the forehead, and one on each palm and on each sole. White body, seated on a lotus throne in crossed-leg position, the left hand holds the stem of a lotus flower, the right hand lowered with the palm out.

Dukor (Kalachakra): The Wheel of Time. 24 arms, each holds a different tantric implement, four faces, two legs, wears tiger skin. Easily confused with Demchok and other wrathful deities: look for consort with both feet on ground.

Guru Rinpoche (Padmasambhava): The guru from India who helped establish Buddhism in Tibet and founded Samya monastery. Pencil-thin moustache and fierce eyes. Holds a *dorje* in his left hand, a skull cup in his right.

Jampa (Maitreya): The Future Buddha either sits or stands, with hands held before his chest in the teaching position. Wears a headdress crown.

Jambeyang (Manjushri): The Bodhisattva of Wisdom sits cross-legged on a lotus throne, though may be standing. Wields a sword in his right hand, and in his left the stem of a lotus flower supporting a prayer text.

King Songtsen Gampo: Creator of Tibetan nation and manifestation of Chenrezig. Sits cross-legged on throne, cradles the wheel of dharma in his left and, right arm extended with thumb and first finger in the symbol of eternity.

Opame (Amitabha): One of the five Dhyani Buddhas, the Buddha of Infinite Light is red, sits in lotus, has both hands in meditative position on his lap.

Palden Lhamo (Sridevi): Protectress of Tibet and the Gelugpa sect. Dark blue, wrathful appearance, often has ritual staff in right hand, skull cup filled with blood in left, and rides a mule with an eye painted on its rump.

Sakyamuni (Sakya Tubpa): Buddha of the Present. Seated in full lotus position, a knob atop his head signifying fiery intelligence, holds an alms bowl in his left hand, right hand touching the earth to signify his enlightenment.

Tamdin (Hayagriva): The alter ego of Chenrezig who destroys demons. Red body, three faces, may have wings and wears a tiger skin. Look for one or more small horse heads atop his own three-faced head.

Tsepame (Amitayus): The Buddha of Long Life is red, wears a crown, sits in lotus, has both hands in lap cradling the vase of life-giving ambrosia.

Tsongkhapa (Je Rimpoche): The 15th-century reformer and founder of the Gelugpa order, and manifestation of Manjushri. Sometimes wears a pointed yellow cap. His left hand grasps the stem of a lotus flower supporting a prayer text, his right holds a lotus flower supporting the sword of wisdom.

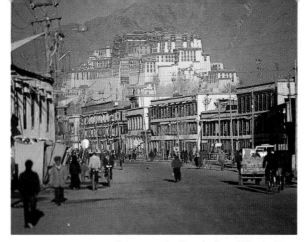

Dawn on the Potala from Lhasa street

6. Hike Around the Lingkor

Gain merit by following pilgrims on the longest of the pilgrimage routes around the city, the Lingkor. For the full effect, start your walk just before dawn; you can eat breakfast later. Allow at least 2 hours for the circuit.

The **Lingkor** circuit (*see map page 34*) lost much of its charm when the path that wended its way among Tibetan houses and shrines was widened and paved years ago, but it still retains some of its magic. Begin your walk on Dekyi Nub Lam at the intersection with Chi Ling Lam.

Just west of the Potala, stroll along the path skirting its western flank. Hundreds of prayer wheels line the walls here; spin them in a clockwise direction with your right hand and murmur *'Om Mani Padme Hum'* which is the prayer ritual written in Sanskrit on each of the wheels. Continue walking and you eventually arrive at Dzuk Trun Lam. Turn right and pause for a few moments at the trees adorned with flags along the banks of Lukhang Lake. This is a good moment to soak in the reflection of the Potala bathed in the glow of the rising sun.

Continue walking past the rows of uninspired new buildings. At the Telecommunications Office at the intersection with Dhode Lam, turn right all the way to Tsang Gyun Shar where you turn right and follow the long road that heads west.

The road eventually parallels the Kyi Chu river. A few minutes past and op-

The Blue Buddha on Chokpori Hill

Reflections of former glory on Lukhang Lake

posite the flag-bedecked bridge leading to Thieves Island, turn right at the end of a long wall. Look for a large pile of offering stones where the pilgrims turn from the road into a walled corridor and follow them.

The path curves left and follows the south base of **Chokpori Hill**. Climb the slight incline and a hundred metres later, you arrive at a cliff face covered in bas reliefs of Buddhas and Bodhisattvas painted in bright, attractive colours.

This venerable shrine is one of the most impressive you will see in Tibet. Pilgrims prostrate themselves before the wall carved with dozens of images. The most important is a large **Blue Buddha**.

From here, the path winds to the west of the hill and ends at Dekyi Nub Lam where you began the circuit. You must be starving by now, so return to your hotel for breakfast.

7. Lukhang Lake

Meditate in a beautiful park while contemplating the reflection of the Potala on the waters of a placid lake.

When the Potala Palace was constructed in 1645, the mortar for its bricks was dug from the ground below the north face of Red

Hill. The resultant pit filled with water, becoming a lake which was dedicated to the *naga* King, a mythical serpent who rules an underworld realm. The Sixth Dalai Lama built a small shrine on an island in the lake to honour the *naga* that once lived in it. Climb to the top floor of the shrine.

The principal image, the *naga* King, is attended by the thousand-armed Tuje Chempo (Mahakarunika) and Drolma (Tara). Of greater interest are the murals with unique depictions of Buddhist subjects. Look at the wall to the left of the altar and you will see ascetics contorted in various yogic positions. The wall behind the altar shows the course of human life from birth to death, anatomy lessons, and the benevolent and malevolent spirits that appear immediately after death. On the right-hand wall are portraits of 84 Indian ascetics demonstrating the various Tantric poses that lead to enlightenment.

The purpose of the visit, however, is to experience the peace of the island on a sun-warmed morning. The *naga* chapel was used as a quiet retreat by several Dalai Lamas.

8. Palhalupuk Cave Temple

An ancient cave temple and yet another spectacular view of the Potala.

Terracotta Buddhas

After breakfast, rent a bicycle and ride along Dekyi Nub Lam to the site of the old western gate that marked the western limits of Lhasa. After cycling a few dozen metres to the east, turn south down a narrow dirt road that leads along the eastern face of Chokpori Hill to the **Palhalupuk Cave Temple** (open daily 9.30am–6pm), with its prayer wheels and friendly monks.

The Palhalupuk is perhaps the oldest religious site in Lhasa, predating the arrival of King Songtsen Gampo in the 7th century. Most its images are bas reliefs which have been carved into the cave wall and painted in bright colours. The central image is that of Sakyamuni; on the right of the back wall is a stone carving of Palden Lhamo (Sridevi), the guardian goddess of Lhasa and the Gelugpa sect. A protective deity, she has a wrathful appearance, holding a ritual staff in her right hand and a skull cap filled with blood in her left while sitting astride a mule. Above Palhalupuk to the right is a temple associated with the Ani Shugseb nunnery.

Visit the Palhalupuk less for its art, of which there is little, than for a superb view of the Potala. As you return to the main road, pause to watch carvers chipping away at *mani* stones, inscribing the ubiquitous *mantra* or prayer, *'Om Mani Padme Hum'* ('Oh Hail to the Jewel in the Lotus').

Lhasa

→ Kathmandu

A drive across Tibet is a journey across the moon. To the weary traveller, the landscape will look like infinite variations of the colour brown. During the rainy season, the valleys are carpeted in green barley that ripens in the late summer sun and mirrors its golden sheen. Trees become clouds of green until autumn, when leaves flutter in brilliant yellows, oranges and reds.

The roads are rough and dusty but worth every kilometre. The following excursions start from Lhasa and go to Tsetang, Samye, Gyantse, Shigatse and across the Nepal border to Kathmandu. There are 10 different excursions, each taking a day or less to com-

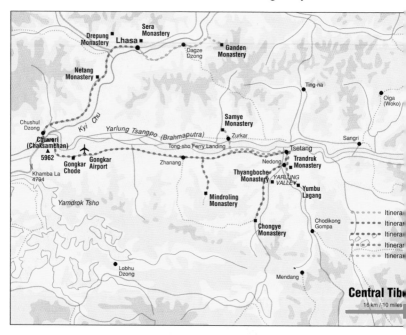

Central Tibe
16 km / 10 miles

Yumbu Lagang, castle in the sky

plete as described. Consider spending at least 5–7 days driving from Lhasa to Kathmandu to enjoy Tibet's unique treasures and natural beauty. If you were to do every itinerary as described, plan on taking 9–10 days. If you are in a hurry, the trip can be completed in two to three very long days, road conditions permitting.

9. Lhasa to Tsetang

Onward to Tsetang (Zetang) with stops at two rural monasteries, Gongkar Chode and Mindroling.

The road to Tsetang (Zetang) in the Yarlung Valley, 195km (121 miles) from Lhasa, is a journey through Tibet's early history. Retrace your route from Lhasa to **Gongkar (Gonggar) Airport**. Before reaching the airport, look for the Gongkar Chode monastery on the right about 200m (220yds) beyond the KM75 marker.

Gongkar Chode provides not only a look at a rural monastery but is a reminder of grimmer times in Tibet. The dark chapels seem imbued with an air of dank emptiness that is exacerbated by the damage that has been done to them. A broad courtyard leads to a portico with murals defaced by speeches of Mao Tse Tung scrawled across them. During the Cultural Revolution (1966–76), the **Assembly Hall**

Take the high road

49

Temple atop Songsten Gampo's tomb

was turned into a barley silo. At the back of the hall are copies of several images of Sakya Pundit and Sakya Gongkar Dorje Tombu. The chapel behind the hall has been rebuilt with a new image of Sakyamuni, which was removed during the post-1959 period.

The monastery's prime appeal is in the chapel to the left of the Assembly Hall. The dim, candle-lit Tantric **protector chapel** is made even gloomier by the 16th-century murals which cover its walls. Their subject is gruesome sky burials. On the right wall, tortured souls are ripped to shreds by dogs, a sign that they are destined for hell. On the opposite wall, a bird removes the heart from a corpse, indicating that it is going to heaven. A second door leads into an inner chamber so dark that the images' features are barely discernible. A Sakyamuni image dominates the altar with an image of Palden Lhamo in the far corner.

An outside stairway leads to a second floor walkway encircling the skylight over the Assembly Hall. Walk to the front chapel, the **Yidam Lhakhang**, whose principal image is Sakyamuni. Of greater interest are the murals portraying Tantric deities and the monastery as it once looked. The third floor is a warren of small rooms, including the bedroom of the present Dalai Lama. A narrow wooden stairway leads to the roof and two large incense burners. Beyond the parapet is a superb view into the courtyard, the adjacent village and the Tsangpo Valley. If you have left Lhasa late in the morning, stop at a Gongkar tea shop for lunch. Otherwise, press on.

The road skims along the edge of the Tsangpo river valley, passing Gongkar Airport 15km (9 miles) after the turnoff for Gongkar Chode. Continue along the incredibly wide and braided Tsangpo river; in places its waters are calm as those of a lake's. Several broad, fertile tributary valleys enter the Tsangpo from the south, each with a fairly large village near the road with Chinese and Tibetan restaurants, guesthouses and small shops selling various snacks, soft drinks and beer.

About 66 km (41 miles) past the Gongkar Chode turnoff is the Drachi valley, the fifth of these big valleys to the east of the Chushul Bridge, where Mindroling is located. Turn right at the dirt road near the KM81 post and drive about 8km (5 miles) along the main valley and up a side valley to **Mindroling Monastery**, one of the two great Nyingmapa monasteries in Central Tibet (the other is Dorje Drak, located farther upstream on the opposite shore of the Tsangpo).

Founded in 1676 by Terdak Lingpa, a famous Nyingmapa 'treasure finder' of religious texts and a teacher of the Fifth Dalai Lama, Mindroling has not been treated kindly over the years; it was razed by the Mongols in 1718 and extensively damaged by the Red Guards. It has risen from the ashes both times and today houses 30 monks. Its scholarly reputation served as a magnet for monks from as far north and east as Amdo and Kham, and it soon became one of Central Tibet's largest and most important religious universities.

Unlike most other burnt umber monasteries, **Mindroling** blends into the hillsides from which its brown stone walls were quarried. The interior holds the statue of its founder and a throne for its incarnate *lama* who now lives in India. The small stupa contains the relics of a recalcitrant monk who died in jail in 1959 for his opposition to Chinese occupation. In the small chapel to the left are two statues of Sakyamuni and Guru Rinpoche (Padmasambhava). The chapel behind the main hall contains Sakyamuni; the head is original but the body has been restored. The other images in the room are also re-creations.

Don't linger too long here if you plan to reach **Tsetang (Zetang)** by evening as the drive takes about 2 hours. Retrace your route back down the Drachi valley to the main paved road and turn right for Tsetang, 42km (26 miles) to the east. Again the road

Tsetang market

parallels the Tsangpo river, and around the KM100 marker, huge sand dunes rear up like raging surf. Soon the valley narrows, the road moves away from the river and numerous buildings begin to line the roadside as you enter Tsetang.

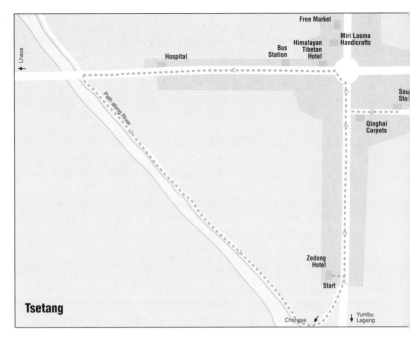

Tsetang

Tsetang (translated as Playground) is one of those towns only a bureaucrat could love. A broad main street runs between drab buildings. Turn left to the **free market**, and right to the Zetang Hotel. It is not a town that invites you to stroll but if you have time before dinner, walk from the hotel into town. Just before you reach the roundabout, make a right into a side street lined with stalls selling garishly-coloured Qinghai carpets and beyond on the left, a small government souvenir store.

At the roundabout, turn left and pause on the sidewalk of shoe-makers. If you are adventurous, continue walking past the bus station until you come to a small river, then turn left along a path beside the bank. Walk through the fields to your hotel as the sun is setting behind the Gibraltar-like mountain etched against the sky to the west. Tsetang is the hub for the following three side trips (*Itineraries 10–12*).

10. Chongye Valley and Thyangboche Monastery

Excursion to Chongye Valley, the ancient capital of the Yarlung kings, and the murals at the Thyangboche Monastery.

Chongye (Qonggyai) Valley, the Valley of the Kings, lies 30km (19 miles) southwest of Tsetang. The road hugs the base of the valley wall before entering the town of **Shol**. It turns left in front of a handsome municipal building, crosses a small river and about 1km (½ mile) later arrives at the foot of a tall mound in a small village. Note that the houses have mud-brown walls with white tops, and black turrets. Climb the path along the stone walls past the donkeys and yaks to the summit.

Below you was the ancient capital of the Yarlung kings who established the Tibetan nation sometime before the 5th century. What you are looking at, in fact, is nothing; everything created from dust has long since returned to dust. Songtsen Gampo established his court here but apparently found it too remote to rule a kingdom and barely a year later moved to Lhasa. The area's symbolic significance, however, remained paramount so that for more than a century, kings continued to be entombed here.

Arrayed before you are the burial mounds of 11 of the 13 kings entombed here. The large one directly in front of you holds Songtsen Gampo's grandson and successor, Mangsong Mangtsen. That of Repachen is on the left, guarded by a small memorial. Langdarma is to his right and Trisong Detsen is on the other side of the tall hill that forms the backdrop for the tombs. Most were looted by marauding warlords after Langdarma's reign. A famous nunnery, **Tseringjon**, is barely visible halfway up the hill.

You are standing on Songtsen Gampo's tomb and, some scholars say, those of his two foreign queens. The nearby chapel, rebuilt in 1983, holds statues of the monarch, his two wives and his two principal ministers. Walk to your left past the reddish, unused chapel to look out on Shol. High on the hill behind the town is the rubble of **Chingwa Tangtse Dzong**, birthplace of the Fifth Dalai Lama. To the left is **Riwo Dechen Monastery** with a chapel built by the Fifth Dalai Lama. To the right are more ruins of the original monastery. In Shol is a jade carving factory which you can tour. Stop for lunch in one of the Tibetan restaurants and try *thukpa*, a hearty noodle soup with meat, or steamed *momo* dumplings.

On the return drive to Tsetang, turn right about 10km (6 miles) after leaving Shol and drive 3km (4 miles) to the base of the hill. Founded in the 7th century, **Thyangboche Monastery** gained prominence only in the 11th century. The great Indian teacher Atisha lived here for a short while but all relics – a small statue of him and a set of manuscripts he had brought from India – disappeared during the Cultural Revolution.

The prime reason for a visit are the fine murals in the **Assembly Hall**. Painted in 1915, they have survived all depredations and glow with colour and superb detail. They are devoted to nearly the entire pantheon of Buddha manifestations and deities. An adjacent chapel holds more murals.

Spinning prayers

Relic of a revolution

An excursion to discover Tibet's early history at Yumbu Lagang. Then be fascinated by the legends of Trandruk.

Head towards Chongye but after 4km (2½ miles), take the left fork for the 9-km (5½-mile) drive to **Yumbu Lagang**. The object of the journey is immediately visible high on an escarpment, its square spire thrusting into the sky. Drive through the village, turn left and drive about halfway up the hill. Most drivers park here and let you walk to the summit.

The Yumbu Lagang is another example of destructive energies at work; what you see is a 1984 reconstruction, albeit a good one. The original was larger and if the design suggests a mad Bavarian prince's dream, it is because it was built as a palace – the first fortified house in Tibet – for the first Yarlung king and was only transformed into a monastery in the 7th century. There is evidence of an earlier structure dating from the 2nd century BC.

Enjoy the breathtaking view before you enter the **Assembly Hall**. From the ramparts of this eyrie, you look down on a village, hills, the river, and a road wending its way south. Visualise a desperate midnight journey in 1959, a small convoy hurriedly passing below, the lonely figure of the young Dalai Lama heading towards exile in India.

The main hall of this Gelugpa chapel holds images of most of the important figures from Tibet's early history, with Sakyamuni at the centre. Along the left wall are statues of the minister Songtsen Gampo sent to India to study Buddhist scriptures; next is Trisong Detsen, founder of Samye monastery; and Latotori, the 120-year-old, 28th Tibetan king during whose reign scriptures are said to have floated down from the sky and landed onto Yumbu Lagang's tall tower.

In the corner is the legendary traveller who, when asked where he came from, raised his index finger to indicate India beyond the mountains. His gesture was interpreted by Chenrezig's

Gelugpa monks

(Avalokiteshvara's) children to mean he had descended from heaven so they immediately proclaimed him king.

On your journey back to Tsetang, stop at **Trandruk Monastery**, one of the three royal Buddhist temples (along with the Jokhang Temple and Samye Monastery) of King Trisong Detsen in the 8th century, 5km (3 miles) before entering Tsetang. The original temple site was also one of a dozen temples built in the 7th century by King Songsten Gampo in order to pin down a demoness which supposedly reclined across the whole of Tibet; Trandruk is positioned strategically on her left shoulder.

According to the legend, Songsten Gampo's Chinese wife Wencheng proclaimed that a temple be built in this region to maintain control over the demoness. Unfortunately, a lake was located on this site, and within it the evil 5-headed dragon. Songsten Gampo went into retreat, and after summoning terrific powers, commanded a falcon to conquer the dragon and suck the water out of the lake, allowing the temple to be built. In Tibetan, Trandruk means 'Falcon-Dragon'.

Tibetan 'Wheel of Life' mural

The monastery is virtually rebuilt as are its images. The Assembly Hall is unremarkable but the atmospheric chapel behind it holds several interesting statues of Jambeyang (Manjushri) and Guru Rinpoche (Padmasambhava). Along the back wall is the Drolma Karo (White Tara).

Trandruk's treasure occupies a case on the second floor. Peer through the dusty glass to see a *thangka* bearing the portrait of Chenrezig made of 30,000 pearls. Local legend says that a devout *lama* brought a copper Buddha image from India which could speak. When the King of Nyethang and his lovely queen came to see it, the statue surprised the wife by telling her she was very beautiful.

She was so delighted that she returned with gold to adorn the statue. Her gesture so surprised the image that it became speechless. The queen, however, interpreted its silence to mean that her gift had been insufficient to honour such an important deity. Ashamed, she tore apart her crown, using the pearls to make this *thangka*, incorporating gold, diamonds, turquoise and jade.

As you walk back towards town from Trandruk, look for a road bridge on the left, about 1km (½ mile) before the Zetang Hotel, with a small temple nearby decorated with strings of prayer flags strung across the river. This was the former site of a 14th-century iron link bridge, built by the revered bridge builder, Tangton Gyelpo. He is also known as the creator of Tibetan opera.

12. Samye Monastery

A barge-ride across the Yar-lung Tsangpo to the gleaming Samye Monastery.

Unless you are prepared to spend the night, **Samye Monastery** is best visited as a daytrip en route to Tsetang from Lhasa, or as a daytrip out of Tsetang and back. Get an early start in order to reach the **Tong-sho** ferry landing, located between KM89 and 90. Be there by 9.30am to catch the morning ferry, though departure times are fairly irregular. If you have hired a vehicle, have the driver wait. During the dry season, the boat must wind among the sandbars, a voyage that can take you up and down the broad river several times. Although the Tsangpo is less than 3km (2 miles) wide, the trip can take up to an hour.

The boatman deposits you on the banks at **Zurkar** where for another small fee, you board a truck. The 35-minute drive takes you past **five white stupas** built by Trisong Detsen to commemorate the arrival of Guru Rinpoche (Padmasambhava). The five spires are said to represent the great teacher's five fingers. When Trisong Detsen asked him for proof of his powers, Guru Rinpoche stretched forth his hand and fire shot from his fingers.

Samye Monastery's gleaming facade seems almost too festive for its arid setting. It was founded in about 770 after Trisong Detsen invited Indian master Santarakshita to train and ordain Tibet's first seven monks. It was at Samye that the great debate of 799 determined that Tibetan Buddhism would follow the Indian school.

Samye was expanded during the reign of the Fifth Dalai Lama. A victim of the Cultural Revolution, its reconstruction began in 1984 and was completed in 1990. Pause at the entrance to look at two photos, one taken before 1959 and the other in 1982. Also at the entrance hangs one of three bronze bells said to have been cast by Trisong Detsen. The other two, at the Jokhang and Trandruk, disappeared after 1959.

Beneath Samye's golden roof is a large **Assembly Hall** dominated by statues of Atisha and two disciples; key deities and kings are arranged along three walls. In the chapel behind is a beautiful Sakyamuni image

The Yarlung road

flanked by the Eight Bodhisattvas. In the right wall of the Assembly Hall is a door leading to a Tantric Protector chapel.

Leave the Assembly Hall and turn right to enter the **Chenrezig Lhakhang** which contains a lovely bas relief portrait of Chenrezig (Avalokiteshvara) and the images of Guru Rinpoche and Songtsen Gampo. Upstairs is a courtyard, its front walls covered with diagrams depicting how a temple should be built and other esoterica which provide an interesting insight into important monastic matters. In the far left-hand corner is a mural of the fabled land of Shambhala, believed to thrive to the north of Tibet. The chapel across the courtyard is devoted to Guru Rinpoche.

Return to the ground floor, exit the Assembly Hall and turn right. Just outside the door is a tall stele etched with Trisong Detsen's proclamation of Buddhism as Tibet's state religion. Continue beyond the stone walls and across the fields to the **Jampa Ling Lhakhang** to the west. After building it, Trisong Detsen, Guru Rinpoche and court elders met here to discuss the design of the larger complex. Most of this building was destroyed and rebuilt. On either side of the entrance door are faded but original murals.

If you want to stay in Samye, very basic rooms (bring your own sleeping bag) are available in the hotel beside the monastery entrance. There is a Tibetan restaurant across the courtyard. If you are only visiting for the day, the last truck back to the ferry landing departs in the early afternoon. If you do not have a ride waiting on the other side, try asking the drivers of vehicles sitting by the landing, or else try waving down a ride as vehicles pass.

Trucks below a glacier

13. Tsetang to Gyantse

Travel to the summit of Khamba La for views of Yamdrok Tso lake. Continue to Karo La, site of the highest battle fought between the British and Tibetans. Arrive in Gyantse in time for the sunset.

There is plenty to see along this route and a lot of distance to cover. It is 311km (193 miles) to Gyantse (Gyantze), so get an early start from Tsetang (Zetang) to retrace the 124km (77 mile) stretch of road along the Tsangpo river back to the Chushul Bridge. Rising from the foot of the bridge is an imposing mountain called **Chuwori** (Chaksamchari), one of the sacred mountains of Tibet. Note the white ladders rising up its flat surfaces as you pass. Painted by pilgrims, they are said to lead the faithful to heaven.

Almost immediately after the bridge, the road climbs through a series of switchbacks. Along the steep slope you pass abandoned stone buildings painted with white sun and moon symbols. Eventually, you arrive at the summit of the **Khamba La** (4,794m/

15,720ft), 32km (20 miles) past the Chushul Bridge and your first view of the beautiful deep blue-green **Yamdrok Tso**, one of Tibet's largest lakes. As the wind whips through the prayer flags, sit in the lee of a stone cairn and enjoy lunch and the magnificent views of the lake, mountains and valley from which you just ascended.

The road descends to the lake bank, which in spring may be piled high with ice slabs. Beyond **Nagartse,** 209km (130 miles) past Tsetang, the road slowly begins to climb but so imperceptibly that you arrive at **Karo La** (5,010m/16,430ft) almost without knowing it. History's highest battle was fought here in 1904 between the British Younghusband expedition and a band of Tibetan soldiers. Just around a bend on the right is a brilliant glacier seemingly poised to crash down from Mt Nechinghangsang (7,220m/23,690ft).

The hills darken and ingenious brick and mud electric poles make their first appearance. Crossing another pass, you drop into a new valley. Soon the distinctive outline of a hilltop *dzong* (castle) appears and you enter Gyantse itself.

For many people, **Gyantse** is the highlight of the trip. Its lanes still wind, the two-storey houses still look Tibetan, the main street is still a dusty boulevard, and robed horsemen still canter down the streets. In short, it is what you expect all Tibetan towns to be. Gyantse's location at the head of the trade route to Sikkim and Darjeeling, and its role as a central dispersion point for goods from Tibetan cities has made it an important commercial centre. Even today, long after the old trade routes have dried up, Gyantse still has a prosperous air and it remains Tibet's third most important city.

In few other Tibetan towns is an evening walk as pleasant as it is in Gyantse. The dying sun filtered through the willow forests sets the old buildings aglow. Assuming you are staying at Gyangtse Hotel (note there is a second hotel spelt 'Gyantse'), leave the gate to the left. Walk along the main road, following the gentle curve of the ridge and its castle that towers over you to Gyantse's main monastery, the **Pelkor Chode**. Watch the sun climb the walls of the **Gyantse Dzong** and disappear. Twilight fades slowly so on your way back to the hotel, cut across the fields to get a longer perspective of the castle. The large Gyangtse Hotel makes it a prominent landmark and it will be difficult to get lost.

Gyantse at dusk

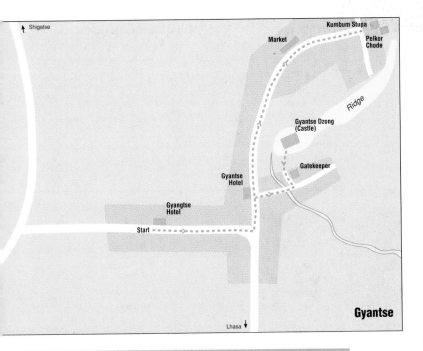

Shigatse ↑

Kumbum Stupa

Market

Pelkor Chode

Ridge

Gyantse Dzong (Castle)

Gatekeeper

Gyantse Hotel

Gyangtse Hotel

Start

Gyantse

Lhasa ↓

14. Gyantse Dzong, Pelkor Chode and Kumbum Stupa

Start off early on your walk up Gyantse Dzong for an overview of Gyantse, then browse in a market. At the far end of town is the Pelkor Chode monastery and Kumbum Stupa, one of Tibet's most revered and unusual masterpieces.

You can drive to the starting point for the climb to **Gyantse Dzong** but it is more interesting to walk. Ask your guide to arrange an early breakfast and an 8.30am start. Before you reach the second Gyantse Hotel (note the difference in spelling) on the left, turn right down a side road, crossing the stream and turning left at the next road. You arrive at the house of the gatekeeper who can open the castle doors. Along the way, notice that Gyantse is a town of walls within walls and that its houses have a more affluent look than elsewhere.

Once inside the castle gates, consider asking your guide to remain behind while you wander on your own. It is better to concentrate on absorbing the atmosphere of this wonderful complex, letting its ghosts guide you as you walk the cobbled, labyrinthine lanes to its peak. At this hour, you may well have it entirely to yourself, so enjoy the views and the solitude.

Yamdrok Tso lake

From a parapet on the south, gaze across the plains and envisage the approach of Younghusband's army. From this height, it is easy to imagine a Tibetan soldier scoffing at the approach of the ant army far below, little suspecting that the puny British soldiers might pose a threat to such an impregnable fortress.

Walk to the opposite ramparts to follow with your eye the watchtower-studded wall that caps the ridge dividing the town. When you are sated, descend to the entrance gate. Turn right at the main road in front of the Gyantse Hotel to enter the central part of town. Rather than drive to the Pelkor Chode, take a stroll through the market to look at butter churns, stirrups, carpets, chests and other accoutrements of farm and nomadic life. Pelkor Chode monastery and the Kumbum Stupa are less than a 10-minute walk farther up the main street at the base of the hills. There are several tea shops and restaurants along here if you feel like a break before visiting the temples.

Restored glory

The **Pelkor Chode**, serving the Gelugpa, Sakya and Buluk (a sub-section of Sakya) orders, was built in 1418 and has survived relatively unscathed to the present day. Its portico is protected by the Guardian Deities of the Four Directions; south, north, east and west. A second entrance bears a beautiful Wheel of Life mural on the right and a lotus symbolising the purity of Buddha's teaching. The door on the left opens into an anteroom leading to a Tantric chapel. The anteroom murals are blackened with smoke and depict sky burials and death. The deities along the front chapel wall include Ekajati and Palden Lhamo. The dance masks along the back wall are worn during dances celebrating the annual *thangka* display. They are very old but even in repose are fierce as the weapons hanging from the beams.

Return to the portico and enter the **Assembly Hall**. Note that the antique *thangkas* hanging from the skylight are woven like tapestries rather than painted. The chapel behind the hall holds some of the most elegantly-crafted images you will see; the dim light only enhances their beauty. The principal images are the Marmese (Dipankara) Buddha of the past, Sakyamuni (present), and Jampa (future). The most striking objects, however, are the small images. Examine the delicate incisions on the silver offering bowls before the Sakyamuni and the superb small bronze Buddhas to their left. If you are here after the Tibetan New Year when they are still

Links to the world

fresh, look at the beautiful medallions the monks have fashioned from *tsampa* and butter.

To the left of the assembly hall, the **Vairocana Lhakhang** holds images of equally fine workmanship including five clay Dhyani Buddhas. The chapel to the right, the **Jampa Lhakhang**, contains a good Jampa image but more interesting is the excellent Nepali-style painting of Chenrezig (Avalokiteshvara).

From the portico, climb the stairway to the second floor. On the left is **Demchok Lhakhang**, whose prized object is a gold and bronze *mandala*. Other fine images include a Dorje Chang and minor Sakya masters and scholars. In the **Jampa Lhakhang**, it is the small Drolma (Tara) that is most cherished by Tibetans. The **Tsongkhapa Lhakhang** at the back contains good murals, and the **Sixteen Arhats** made of lacquered clay in the *lhakhang* dedicated to them are excellent. The small temple at the head of the stairs on the right holds a Sakyamuni. The third floor shrine is dominated by a Sakyamuni Buddha and holds several superb Tantric wheel murals.

As you exit Pelkor Chode, descend the stairs and angle right towards the base of the hill to one of Tibet's most revered and unusual architectural masterpieces, the multi-storied **Kumbum Stupa**, whose protective eyes look beneficently down on pilgrims and the townsfolk. Built in 1440 in the shape of a 108-sided *mandala*, it is distinguished by fine statues and 15th-century murals painted by Nepali artists. Of its 112 chapels, only 23 are open to the public.

The four largest chapels are at the cardinal points and contain Kumbum's four most important Buddha images: Sakyamuni to the south, Opame (Amitabha) to the west, Marmese (Dipankara) to the north, and Jampa to the east. Between each pair are four small chapels containing large images backed by murals.

Climb the entrance stairs to the south chapel, the **Sakyamuni Lhakhang**. Sakyamuni is the central image flanked by two chief disciples. Others include eight Medicine Buddhas and Guru Rinpoche (Padmasambhava). The west chapel, **Sukhavati Lhakhang**, is dedicated to the Pure Land, ruled by Opame, whose manifestation towers over you. The **Marmese Lhakhang**, containing the Buddha of the Past, faces north. The **Tushita Lhakhang** is ruled by Jampa, who resides in the Pure Land until he makes his appearance in the future. Four more small chapels bring you back to the starting point. The upper floors, which are undergoing restoration, can be reached by the stairway between the Four Guardian Kings and the Guru Gonpo Lhakhang along the southeast face of the Kumbum. There are four top floor chapels. At the summit of the structure is the **Dorje Lhakhang** and a superb view of Pelkor Chode and Gyantse town.

15. Gyantse to Shigatse

Journey to Tibet's second largest city, stopping at Drongtse to see remarkable slate bas relief carvings, and Shalu's unique Mongolian architecture with its original 14th-century frescoes inside.

There is plenty of time to see both Drongtse and Shalu en route to Shigatse (Xigaze), 90km (56 miles) away, so take the opportunity to wake up late. Drive south from Gyantse to a T-junction where you turn right towards Shigatse (left goes to India). Far off to the right are the ruins of monasteries and another *dzong* guarding the western approach to Gyantse. Behind you, the Gyantse Dzong looks impressive on its rocky spine.

About 19km (12 miles) from the junction, the **Drongtse Monastery** appears on a hill to the left, near the KM71 post. A single-lane road accessible to vehicles climbs through a series of hairpin turns. Although it has recently been rebuilt, Drongtse is not particularly noteworthy from an architectural point of view. But, it does possess one of the most remarkable collections of slate bas relief carvings in Tibet. Several lie at the base of the flag pole with the re-

A Drongtse monastery carving

mainder on the roof of the chapel at the rear. Once the assembly hall is completed, monks will install them inside. See them now in the fullness of sunlight to appreciate their beauty.

The drive to **Shalu Monastery** and Shigatse winds through fertile farmlands beside the Nyang Chu River. Near the KM18 post, 53km (33 miles) past Drongtse, turn left onto dirt road and drive another 3km (2 miles) into the small village above which the monastery towers. The road crosses a river bed and may be impassable during summer rains.

Shalu Monastery's monks belong to the Buluk sect of the Sakya order. Try to time a visit to coincide with the prayer session at either 9am, 3pm or 6pm. What first strikes you about the monastery is the presence of tall juniper trees shading the courtyard; most Tibetan monastery courtyards do not have trees. Next is the Mongolian appearance of the roof, not just its shape but its green glazed tiles. Donations from wealthy Chinese patrons account for its green tiles and Mongolian architectural treatment.

Modern masks

Shalu dates from the 11th century but is associated with the 14th-century Buddhist scholar, Buton, who founded a small order bearing his name. The upper part of the monastery was destroyed in the Cultural Revolution along with a precious 227-volume (another auspicious Buddhist number) copy of the *Tengyur* scriptures which Buton had collated and hand-copied.

Cross the courtyard to see the **West Chapel** which contains a stone Chenrezig (Avalokiteshvara), said to have been carved in Bodhgaya, India, and a statue of Buton himself. The gold and silver stupa is said to contain his remains. Enter the two-storey **South Chapel** whose entrance hall holds three murals, including an astrological map created by Buton based on astronomic propositions, a visual treatise on meditation, and a description of proper attire for monks.

On the walls of the upper floor chapels are numerous paintings of Tantric *mandalas*. Walk to the terrace to look at the roof tiles in detail.

Close examination shows that they are not of *Mongolian roofs of Shalu* similar hue but range from tan to blue. Look also at the finely crafted medallions along the upper and lower edges of the roof.

Shigatse is less than an hour's drive. Return to the main road and turn left; the golden roofs of Tashilhunpo monastery in Shigatse are only 18km (11 miles) away.

The highlight of any trip to Shigatse, Tibet's second largest city, is the striking Tashilhunpo Monastery, renowned as the seat of the Panchen Lama. Then, see how carpets are made at the Shigatse Carpet factory, follow the Lingkor to acquire merit, and browse through the Tibetan market for curios.

Shigatse (Xigaze), whose name translates as Best of the Land, is Tibet's second largest city. Like Lhasa, many of its ancient lanes and quarters have been transformed to serve socialist ends; the resultant look is hardly spiritual. Its streets are broad, the concrete buildings low, and it sprawls rather than bunches like a Tibetan town. Aside from the stunning Tashilhunpo Monastery, there is little other than a lively market to spur one to explore its streets.

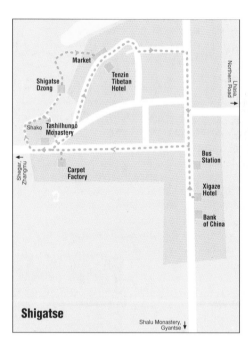

Founded in 1447 by the first Dalai Lama, **Tashilhunpo Monastery** (open daily 9am–noon) is renowned as the seat of the Panchen Lama (Great Teacher), a title first bestowed in 1642 by the Great Fifth on his tutor. Extensive additions were later made to the monastery. Later years saw further expansion so that before 1959, it ranked as one of Tibet's four biggest Gelugpa monasteries with 6,000 monks. Within its walls are the important Tantric and philosophy colleges known as *tratsang*.

From a distance, you can see Tashilhunpo's golden roofs gleam against the steep hillside, but it is the huge *thangka* wall, like a giant drive-in theatre screen, that commands your attention. The monastery is aesthetically pleasing with a broad courtyard, long entryway and massive gate that frames the complex. Tiers of whitewashed buildings lift the eye to the red halls with their gold-sheathed roofs.

From the impressive entrance gates, an-

Tashilhunpo tower

Thangka festival at Tashilhunpo Monastery

gle to your left through the maze of buildings in order to follow the proper clockwise pilgrimage circuit around the monastery. The first temple in this monastic city is the towering, golden-roofed **Jamkhang**, housing an enormous seated image of Jampa (Maitreya), the Future Buddha. The gilded image, which is 26-m (86-ft) tall, including the base, was cast by the Ninth Panchen Lama in 1914 and took nearly 4 years to complete. The body was cast with over a hundred tons of copper and brass, and the exterior was gilded with nearly 300kg (661lbs) of gold. A temple upstairs allows pilgrims to observe the Jampa's huge face. The other room of interest, with 1,000 small clay images of Tsongkhapa, is at the entrance to the Jamkhang.

Turn left as you leave the Jamkhang, following a stone-walled corridor past the Palace of the Panchen Lamas, which is rarely open to the public, to reach the **Kudung Lhakhang**. Along with the Jamkhang, this large red building is one of the most imposing structures of Tashilhunpo. Inside is the tomb of the Fourth Panchen Lama, Chokyi Gyeltsen, the acclaimed teacher of the Fifth Dalai Lama who was honoured by being declared an incarnation of Opame (Amitabha), the Buddha of Infinite Light. He was also the first to receive the title of Panchen Lama, but because the three previous abbots of Tashilhunpo received this same title posthumously, he is now known as the fourth in this lineage. A large silver *stupa* within this temple enshrines his remains.

Farther up to the left, along a tall red wall, the corridor leads to the impressive courtyard of **Kelsang Lhakhang**, Tashilhunpo's largest complex of temples. The oldest building here is the **Dukhang Assembly Hall** on the left, built in the 15th century by Gedun

Drub, the First Dalai Lama. The hall provides your first view of a monastery as it would have looked prior to 1959; the contrast with rebuilt monasteries and re-created images is striking. One of the original buildings of Tashilhunpo, it was spared because of its historic association with the Chinese. It retains the richness and high artistry of a bygone age with its tall, stout tree trunk pillars, bound in iron straps and decorated with beautiful brass plaques and bas relief floral motifs. At the front sits the huge throne of the Panchen Lama. Breathe in the atmosphere before moving into the chapel located behind the altar.

The chapel, the oldest in Tashilhunpo, was also built by the First Dalai Lama. It is distinguished not only by its images but by the beautiful brass frames in which they rest, and the very ornate bowls on the altar. The central image of Sakyamuni is flanked by two disciples while in front are five images of (from left) the First Dalai Lama, a disciple of Tsongkhapa, Tsongkhapa himself, another disciple, and the Fourth Panchen Lama. The smaller chapel, the **Drolma Lhakhang**, to the right, was also built by the First Dalai Lama and is dedicated to Drolma (Tara).

Upstairs on the second floor is the **Tuwang Donden Lhakhang**, one of the most revered temples at Tashilhunpo. Here is the bejewelled burial *stupa* of Gedun Drub, founder of the monastery and the only Dalai Lama not to be enshrined in Lhasa at the Potala Palace, and the *stupas* of the Second and Third Panchen Lamas.

Descend the stairs and exit the Dukhang Assembly Hall. As you face the courtyard, turn left and begin the clockwise circuit around the temples surrounding this beautiful enclosure. The first temple is the newest addition at Tashilhunpo, a towering gold-roofed shrine which was completed in 1988 with the 10th Panchen Lama presiding over the opening ceremonies just 6 days before he died. It holds the remains of the Fifth through Ninth Panchen Lamas whose bodies were hidden during the Cultural Revolution. All the remains were placed in a single tomb as the identity of each had been confused.

The statue in the middle is that of the Ninth Panchen Lama. A new shrine and burial *stupa* has been completed which now contains the body of the 10th Panchen Lama.

The hall seems designed to overwhelm by its sheer size. This extends to the enormous polished turquoise and other stones set in huge silver bases on which the images rest. Its gaudiness is offset some-

Yak country

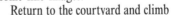
Fields ablaze with flowers

what by fine *mandalas* painted on the ceiling. Murals on the upper floor depict the lives of the Panchen Lamas.

Continue clockwise around the courtyard to the **Jokhang temple** whose Sakyamuni is attended by 1,000 small Buddha images. The next, dedicated to Dorje Chang, holds two silver *stupas*. Two doors down is the entrance to a printing studio on the left. Its walls are lined by wood blocks carved with Buddhist scriptures. Under the dust-frosted windows, monks patiently ink the blocks, cover them with rough paper and then press in the ink with a roller. You can buy sheets of scriptures as well as bright prayer flags for a few yuan apiece.

At the end of the hallway, turn right through three narrow gallery-chapels dedicated to Sakyamuni, Drolma Jang (Green Tara), and Tsongkhapa, each attended by a thousand smaller images.

Stairways lead to similar gallery and chapel arrangements. On the third floor, above the printing studio, is the **Kangyur Lhakhang**. Old monks chant *sutras* requested and paid for by visiting pilgrims. Of the galleries here, the second, the **Ganden Lhakhang** is the most interesting. Its central image, cast in bronze by Indian masters, is that of Tsongkhapa attended by the Sixth and Eighth Panchen Lamas. Beyond the chapel is the **Drolma Lhakhang** with some fine images.

Happy pilgrims

Return to the courtyard and climb the stairs opposite the Assembly Hall to a series of small chapels. The first holds a *stupa* and a lovely embroidered *thangka* honouring Dorje Jigche. The next contains an image of Jowo Sakyamuni and the last, that of Jampa. On the floor directly above are chapels dedicated to Drolma, the Fourth Panchen Lama and Jampa. The end room honours Tsongkhapa.

Descend to the ground floor and cross to the opposite side, bypassing a protector chapel to the **Jampa chapel** beside it. It contains the head of a fine Jampa whose body rests on the floor downstairs. Upstairs, a Sakyamuni sits amidst fierce Tantric *thangkas* and two stuffed snakes, odd companions for such an exalted deity.

From the Kelsang courtyard complex, exit via a corridor running alongside the Dukhang and under several of the temples, jog right and then left to return to the main alley leading back to the

Breaking camp

monastery entrance. Descend a little way, then turn left into the **Ngagpa Tratsang Tantric College**, which more than any other building has preserved its antique atmosphere. If you are fortunate, you will arrive as drums are beating, horns are sounding and chants are rising to the heavens on fragrant juniper smoke. Go up the stairs into the old, dark assembly hall where monks gather in the mornings for prayer ceremonies. The main statue is Tsongkhapa, flanked by his two disciples and the Fourth Panchen Lama.

The next main building on the left down along the main alley is the **Tsenyi Tratsang Philosophy and Debate College**. Most mornings, monks gather in this tree-lined inner courtyard practising their debating techniques, enthusiastically slapping their right hand into their left as they display their knowledge of Buddhist philosophy to their fellow monks. There is an Assembly Hall on the ground floor of the college and three protector shrines upstairs.

Follow the main alley farther down to finish the monastery circuit and return to the tall entrance gate. Several restaurants across the street are frequented by pilgrims, making them fascinating places to take a break or have lunch. Return to your hotel, or head back into town to shop for antiquities in the **Tibetan covered market**.

Your next stop is **Shigatse Carpet Factory** just across the road, one of the many self-help business projects initiated by the Tenth Panchen Lama. He invited Lobsang Gelek, a noted Tibetan businessman living in India to return to Tibet to manage it. Gelek was well chosen for this position, having achieved acclaim in the early 1960s when he was asked to start the first carpet factory in Kathmandu as part of a Swiss financial aid project to assist Tibetan refugees in Nepal. The carpet project grew beyond anyone's dreams and is now lauded as the most successful aid project ever established. Considering the tenor of the times, it is to Gelek's credit that he did so and in a short time has made a success of it. Opened in 1987, it now employs 230 Tibetans.

The factory carries out all the dyeing and weaving on the premises and invites visitors to see how Tibetan carpets are made. Some carpets are coloured with natural dyes blended from stones, barks and woods; others are chemically dyed.

Making wool carpets

One of the charms of this weaving studio are the lilting, high-pitched songs sung by the women as they thump wooden mallets to firm the weft into the warp. The designs are traditional but the craftsmanship is still in the formative stages and does not approach the quality produced by the Kathmandu factories.

Turn left from the carpet factory and walk to the main road, facing the Tashilhunpo entrance gate. The pilgrims' walk around the monastery begins about 200m (220 yds) farther up the main road to the left.

Like the circuit around Lhasa, the pilgrim's route (called the Lingkor) around Tashilhunpo brings blessings to those who tread it. Follow the pilgrims down the street to the corner of the whitewashed wall and turn right between the wall and a small village. As you pass, turn the prayer wheels and breathe in the juniper incense. A short way up the hill, you will encounter a man displaying dozens of small medallions. He has acquired merit by pressing clay into moulds and sun-baking them. At the corner, turn right and head along the upper wall. Wheeling high above you are griffon vultures, indicating the presence of a sky burial site beyond the tall hill. Resist the impulse to peek; this is strictly off-limits.

Halfway along, almost directly behind the new temple, the path runs between a large boulder and a rocky outcrop festooned with wool, prayer flags and banners. On the near side of the boulder is a tiny hole framed by etched scriptures. Tibetans claim that if you stand one pace from the rock, close your eyes and successfully poke your finger into the hole, all your wishes will come true.

At the far corner of the

Pilgrim circuit around Lingkor

A monastery door

Lingkor is the huge wall on which the giant *thangka* is hung each July. You will notice that it is in fact a narrow building, the interior holding ancient sacred scriptures. Just beyond, the path splits at a small shrine. Turning right will take you downhill along the eastern wall and back to the gate. It is more interesting, however, to continue straight.

The path runs level along the brow of the hill and after a short way, you see the ruined **Shigatse Dzong**, whose shape has earned it the sobriquet of the Small Potala. The longer Lingkor route passes behind the *dzong* before dropping into the market. If you are not up to the challenge of the walk, turn right at the stone cairn and follow the zigzag path into the town below. The **market** bustles with vendors offering a selection of souvenir items that rival Lhasa's Barkor Square.

17. Shigatse to Shegar

Journey from Shigatse to Sakya Monastery, reminiscent of a medieval European monastery. Relax with a soak at a spa, experience panoramic views from Lakpa La pass, and end the day in the fortress town of Shegar (Xegar).

A long day of travel, covering 279km (173 miles) and many high passes which separate Shigatse from Shegar (Xegar). Start by 8.30am in order to visit Sakya Monastery along the way. Consider taking Diamox in the morning (see pages 96–97 for potential side effects) as you will cross the highest pass of your journey across Tibet.

Once out of Shigatse, you will cross a painted desert striated in pastel hues. House exteriors have trios of short vertical stripes which descend from the roofline. The broad bands – red on the left, black on the right and a third one between them understood as white are a symbolical tribute to the three protecting bodhisattvas of Tibet.

From time to time along the roadside you will see mud-con-

Sakya's shrine

structed thrones, often flanked by twin incense furnaces. The Panchen
Lama sat on them to deliver sermons when he visited the area in
1986. The hillsides above villages are often marked by huge '*Om
Mane Padme Hum*' chants written on white stones.

As the road leaves the broad valleys and begins the climb to the
Tsho La (Tsuo La), the hills are almost verdant. Villages are small
clusters of a few houses huddled against the brisk winds.

The **Tsho La** at 4,500m (14,760ft) is marked by a rock cairn
that offers views into valleys on both sides, but lacks the splen-
dour of other Tibet passes. The road descends into the valley town
of **Renda**, distinguished by houses with black window frames. Just
beyond the Sakya Bridge, turn left on an unmarked road that leads
26km (16 miles) to **Sakya Monastery**.

Sakya exudes the atmosphere of a lunar city, its starkness un-
derscoring the desolateness of the landscape. The monastery and
the town are distinguished by a unique colour scheme: grey-black
buildings with white stripes delineating the roofline, and red and
white bands running vertically along the face of each building. Its

sombreness gives it the air of a
medieval European monastery.

Sakya was established in 1073
by Kongchok Gyalpo, scion of
a powerful family, whose son
was one of the first seven Tibetan monks ordained at Samye.
It was a non-celibate monkhood
whose leadership passed from
father to son, and which ruled
both ecclesiastical and secular
affairs with a firm hand. It was
from here that the Mongols in
1247 plucked the abbot, Sakya

The white-striped walls of Sakya

Pundit, to rule Tibet. The 108-chapel northern monastery across the
river above the village was destroyed during the Cultural Revolution. Only the **Vijaya Lhakhang** and a forlorn *stupa* have survived.

The exclusive nature of the Sakya order is reflected in the
monastery's austere, forbidding architecture. The windowless south-

ern complex anchors one corner of the town. A long, narrow passage shielded by a tall wall against blowing sand
leads from the street to a large courtyard holding four
chapels and an enormous Assembly Hall.

Just inside the courtyard, turn left and climb the stairs
to the **Phuntsok Palace** on the second floor. These chambers serve as the residence of one of the two Sakya abbots. Here are found several Drolma (Tara), Tsepame
(Amitayus) and Sakya Pundit statues but the central image is of Jambeyang (Manjushri). Return to the courtyard and walk clockwise to the **Jambeyang Lhakhang**

which is dominated by the images of Jowo Sakyamuni and Jambeyang, both said to have been sculpted by Sakya Pundit.

The interior of Sakya's **Assembly Hall** is as sombre as its exterior. Thick pillars, each made of a single tree trunk, and an array of massive images dwarf and overwhelm the viewer. They serve as a reminder of the Buddha's teachings and as reliquaries for the remains of Sakya notables. Equally impressive are the enormous, finely-worked silver and brass frames around the images.

The large Buddha on the back wall holds relics of Sakya Pundit while in the corner is the *stupa* of the 27th ruler of Sakya, whose son now lives in Seattle, US. There is an image of Sakya Kunga Nyingpo, one of the founders of Sakya, as well as the tomb of the 13th Sakya king. The murals on the back wall portray the previous lives of the Buddha.

From the courtyard, proceed to the chapel on your left. Called the **Nguldung Lhakhang** (Chapel of the Silver Stupas) for its 11 reliquaries of Sakya luminaries, it holds numerous tomes prepared by Sakya scholars. A door leads to a second, smaller chapel with an image of Sakya Pundit seated in discussion with Manjushri.

The final room, the **Drolma Palace**, is reached via stairs that begin in the courtyard entrance, leading to a second floor residence for the Sakya abbots. One of the complex's most interesting rooms, it holds five stupas containing relics of previous lamas. Beautifully rendered murals depict the life of Guru Rinpoche (Padmasambhava) on the left wall.

From Sakya to Shegar, the road runs west through more dusty and desolate scenery, so it is with a sense of relief that 11km (7 miles)

before **Lhatse** (Lhaze), a sign in Chinese advertises a spa. Located 400m (440yds) off the road to the right is a green-roofed white building that invites travellers to soak themselves in mineral water. Suitably refreshed, continue on the road to Lhatse, your lunch stop. Among its square buildings hunkered next to the road are several Chinese restaurants. Nearly

Mustards abloom in Lhatse Valley

3km (2 miles) beyond Lhatse, the road forks to the left and ascends through more inhospitable terrain than any you have so far encountered. Sheets of shale define the mountains, most of which stand on end with jagged pinnacles pointing to the sky.

The twisting road eventually arrives at the highest point of the entire journey, **Lhakpa La**, also called the **Jia Tsuo La** (5,220m/17,120ft), and the first extensive view of the northern faces of the world's highest mountains. About 10km (6 miles) down the road, look for the white wedge of Mt Everest (Chomolungma).

Approximately 50km (31 miles) beyond the pass, turn right for the 5-km (3-mile) drive into Shegar.

Shegar, also called New Tingri, is another town that lies in the shadow of the White Crystal Castle, the great fortress of **Shegar Dzong**, the former residence of the local governor. Completely destroyed in the Cultural Revolution, it is majestic even in ruins. Seeming to grow out of the craggy brown rock, its sinuous wall bristles with watchtowers that resemble stegosaurs spines.

In 1855, marauding Nepalis in search of booty cut off the *dzong*'s water supply and settled in for a long siege. Supposedly, clever Tibetan monks and soldiers boiled yak butter until it separated. Making a great display of painting the fortress walls with the white liquid, the Tibetans duped the Gurkhas into thinking that the fortress must have a secret spring that allowed its defenders to be so profligate with their water as to use it to whitewash the walls. After a month, the Gurkhas called off their siege and returned home empty-handed.

The first mountaineers allowed in Tibet to attempt Mt Everest, the 1921 British Mt Everest Reconnaissance Expedition, marvelled at the grandeur of Shegar Dzong, below which they established their first base camp en route to attempting the world's highest peak.

Shegar proper has little to recommend except the highest post office in China. If this impresses you, mail a postcard home. Its principal attraction is the hilltop fortress, the old village at its foot, and the **Shegar Chode** halfway up its flanks.

You will most likely arrive in Shegar by late evening after the long and exhausting drive from Shigatse. After dinner, pull out your star map and experience a night sky as you may never have seen before. If you are staying at the Shegar Guest House, climb up the iron rungs to the flat roof, lie back and gaze into the sky. You will understand how the Milky Way came to be so named.

Shegar Dzong

Sanskrit mantras

18. Shegar to Kathmandu

Climb up Shegar Chode early in the morning to observe monks at their prayers. Wind through wondrous scenery, including spectacular panoramas of the Himalaya, stopping at Milarepa's Cave. After border formalities at Zhangmu and Kodari, travel the final leg to Kathmandu.

The 358km (222 miles) from Shegar (Xegar) to Kathmandu can be completed in one rather long day, depending on road conditions. The Chinese Customs and Immigration post in Zhangmu closes at 6pm. If you are running late, consider staying in Zhangmu, or near the Nepal border post in Kodari or Tatopani villages.

After an early breakfast, drive into town. Opposite the second bridge is an open area, and in the right-hand corner is a path leading to **Shegar Chode**, winding through narrow alleys of painted doors. After climbing above the village, the path levels off, giving you a superb view down of the morning activities on the flat roof terraces and the enclosed courtyards normally hidden by high walls.

Climb through a tall gateway and up the hill to the Shegar Chode's forecourt. In the chill morning air, monks pad barefooted to the **Assembly Hall** to chant their prayers. Shegar Chode was founded in 1266 by Sindeu Rinchen, a local Gelugpa monk who built 25 chapels housing Gelugpa, Nyingmapa, Kadampa, Sakyapa, Buton, and even Bon monks. Not long after the Fifth Dalai Lama visited Shegar Chode, the monastery converted to the Gelugpa order. Those monks who did not concur – several sects allow monks to marry but Gelugpa was celibate – were compelled to leave. Shegar Chode eventually became a sub-monastery of Sera. The monastery was razed in 1965 and only rebuilt in 1985. While the complex is based on the original design, there are fewer chapels because out of the 300 monks before 1959, there are now only 30.

The Assembly Hall is dark with light falling in patches from the skylight high overhead. Most of the monastery's principal images are in the **Chogun Lhakhang**, behind the Assembly Hall. At the centre is Tsongkhapa flanked by two disciples and behind him is Dorje Chang. In a second chapel behind the first are three images of Gelugpa lamas.

If you feel like exercising and are in good physical condition, scaling the hill to the top of **Shegar Dzong** provides a view of Mt Everest. A trail ascends the hill to the back of the fortress and eventually scrambles to the summit. Or you can wait to drive the additional 60km (37 miles) farther west to old Tingri to see this mountain from the window of your vehicle.

From Shegar, drive 5km (3 miles) back to the main road and turn right for the border and Nepal; 7km (4 miles) farther on is a police post where officials conduct a cursory check of your passport and other travel documents. The stream flowing under the

North facade of Mt Everest

bridge just beyond the checkpoint is the upper Arun River, which eventually becomes a mighty body of water slicing through the Himalaya on its journey through Nepal to join the Ganges in India.

Continue on the main road through striking terrain, the realm of herders and nomads. About 50km (31 miles) down the road is **Old Tingri**, a small village with historical links to the Sherpas of Nepal who are just across the Tingri

Prayer flags

Plains and the Nangpa La pass. Beyond a tall hill, you are confronted with the full panorama of the Himalaya, the most spectacular view of your journey. The pyramidal peak on the far left is Mt Everest (Chomolungma) at 8,848m (29,028ft).

Gutsuo, 38km (24 miles) farther on, is the best place to photograph Everest. Look for it over your right shoulder, the tallest and most impressive peak on the horizon. Beyond the intersection with the road west to Kyirong at KM5265, you begin to climb. As you do, the full glory of the Himalaya seems to rise out of the bare yellow earth. At **Lalung La**, or **Thang La**, (5,050m/ 16,560ft), the world's highest peaks seem within touching distance. Drive on, dropping into the heart of the mountains that tower to impossible heights, so tall that you must crouch down to see their summits out of the vehicle windows. Another 50km (31 miles) down the ravine and 200m (220yds) before KM5233, you arrive at a small village of stone houses before Nyelam.

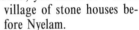

Travelling the Lhasa-Kathmandu Road

Nearby is **Milarepa's Cave,** where the mystic poet-monk meditated. Thread your way through the village and then descend the steep slope to the monastery on your left. Milarepa, a disciple of the teacher Marpa, chose the ascetic path rather than join a monastery, meditating at various sites between Mt Everest and Mt Kailas. He finally settled in this cave where he later died. The original monastery was founded in the reign of the Fifth Dalai Lama and it has been rebuilt with what appears to be limited funds. The Assembly Hall is small and all of the images are new. Milarepa is portrayed in a mural on the right-hand wall.

Outside the door on your right are three stone slabs bearing shallow impressions. The largest is said to be where Milarepa sat as he meditated. Beside it is Milarepa's footprint and behind it, the hoof print of Palden Lhamo's horse. The front lip of the cave is supported by two large boulders. According to popular belief, Milarepa decided the cave needed a larger entrance, which required raising the roof. He asked a disciple to find a boulder the size of a yak. The required stone was inserted but the roof was still too low. Milarepa then sent the disciple after a second rock the size of a

The gorge to Nepal

sheep. It was set atop the 'yak' stone and Milarepa had a new meditation cell.

Climb back to the road and continue to **Nyelam**, 11km (6¾ miles) down the road. A small trading town wedged between a river and a hillside, Nyelam has the look of recent, haphazard growth. There is a hotel (Snowland) and several good restaurants should you wish to break your journey.

Beyond Nyelam, the scenery becomes even more spectacular; you feel you really are part of the Himalaya itself. The road drops precipitously – 1,450m (4,757ft) in 33km (20 miles) – zigzagging down a gorge road scored into steep walls. A new unfamiliar colour appears – green. Trees, grass and shrubs cling to the steep slopes.

Built in 1969, the road sometimes washes out in the rainy season and can be blocked by snow in the winter. The Chushan Hotel, halfway between Nyelam and Zhangmu was built to accommodate stranded guests while the road is cleared.

By the time you reach **Zhangmu** (or Khasa to the Nepalis), 242km (150 miles) from the Shegar turnoff, most evidence of Tibet is gone, replaced by Nepali wooden houses and Chinese cement buildings. Zhangmu hangs on a cliff face, its boom town architecture having a temporary look; even the monastery roofs are sheathed in corrugated iron sheets. Gone are the yaks and your trip is truly coming to an end.

But not quite. You still have to get to Kathmandu. There are no less than 8km (5 miles) of steep no man's land between the Chinese checkpoint at Zhangmu and Nepali immigration just north of Kodari at Tatopani. The Chinese customs post opens from 10am–6pm, Chinese time. First your passport will be stamped at the immigration counter, then your baggage will be inspected by the customs officials. Typically, they may ask what you have purchased in Tibet and China, in particular, books or printed literature that have anything to do with the Dalai Lama or the Tibetan exile community. Once everything is in order, try to find a vehicle to catch a ride

Look out for zigzagging paths

Chinese-built bridge

down to the **Friendship Bridge** across to the Nepal border. Sitting atop a truck loaded with goods bound for Nepal is usually all that is available, if there is any traffic at all. Otherwise, hire porters for 100 Nepali rupees each to carry your baggage down the steep slope. Keep an eye on your porters; there have been more than a few incidents of luggage and porters that never showed up at the bottom. Walking is not recommended for the unfit. The porters normally take shortcuts down steep, rock-strewn paths that cut across bends in the road. The path drops 530m (1,700ft) in 8km (5 miles) and it takes just over an hour to get to the bridge.

Nepal is 2¼ hours behind Beijing so you still have time to make it to Kathmandu before dark. The Nepalese border post at **Kodari** is said to be open 24 hours a day, but just in case, it's a good idea to go through during daylight hours. A 15- or 30-day Nepalese visa can be obtained here. A 24-hour transit visa can be had if you can show an onward ticket. If you plan to stay on in Nepal, tourist visas can now be extended in Kathmandu for up to 5 months each calendar year.

From Kodari, travel agencies can arrange a vehicle to pick you up after you have cleared customs. This is certainly the most convenient way, but also the most expensive at about US$100 for the 4-hour drive to your Kathmandu hotel.

The alternative is to find your own way back, usually not a problem unless it is late at night, or the road has been blocked below by landslides; not an uncommon event during the monsoon months of July and August. Look for taxis and buses 50m (150ft) down the road from the Nepalese customs building. Taxis to Kathmandu can be hired at a flat rate of about US$40, but try bargaining. Alternatively, split the fare if there are four of you. The local bus is cheaper, and slower. There are numerous unscheduled buses and jeeps during the day to Barabise, 26km (16 miles) away; some go all the way to Kathmandu. From Barabise, catch one of the buses which run every half hour for the remaining 88km (55 miles) to Kathmandu. There are hotels in Barabise if you need to stay the night, and several good *dal bhat* (traditional Nepalese food of rice, lentils and curried vegetables, or curried chicken or mutton if you ask for it) restaurants if you are hungry.

Tibet Trekking

Athough mountaineering expeditions have been permitted since the 1970s, trekking is still in its infancy in Tibet due to a lack of infrastructure and equipment. The terrain in Tibet and the distances involved do not lend themselves to trekking when compared with the clement climate and variety of terrain available in Nepal and India. Also, you must be prepared to trek with a group in Tibet.

The following itineraries can be gruelling. Make sure that you are physically prepared for the long days of trekking. All the treks can be arranged through overseas or Nepal-based travel agencies working in conjunction with their Lhasa counterparts. Permits will be secured and transportation to base camps, porters and food will be arranged by the trekking agencies. You will find that the best expeditions take along Nepali Sherpas and high-quality equipment to make the trip more comfortable. The optimum trekking period is from May through September when the days are not too cold and the passes are relatively clear of snow.

Lhasa to Samye

This 4-day trek will take you north through the hills south of Lhasa to Samye Monastery, the birthplace of Tibetan Buddhism. It can be included as part of a 12-day Tibetan tour that includes Lhasa and Tsetang (Zetang). In the summer, trekkers will see grasslands, mountains and yaks.

Lhasa to Lake Namtsho

A 4-day trek north to one of Tibet's most famous lakes. Drive to Damshung (Damxung) where you spend the first night. The pickup point is Tashi Do where there is a large bird sanctuary. You also visit several meditation caves.

Everest North Base Camp

An arduous 8- to 10-day trek from Rongbuk (Dza Rongphu) Monastery (4,980m/16,350ft) to the Everest (Chomolungma) Base Camp and above. The road to Rongbuk turns south 12km (7½ miles) past the Shegar junction to Padruchi village and crosses the Zakka Chu River. The intrepid can explore the spectacular glaciers of the highest mountain in the world.

Kharta Valley Trek

This 13-day trek to the east face of Everest is longer and requires more stamina but is a very worthwhile expedition. You will cross the 4,800m (15,750ft) Sha-u Pass to the Kangshung Face Base Camp on the east face of Everest. In the summer, spectacular grassland flowers will be blooming in the remote Kharta valley.

Around Mount Kailas

This demanding but classic drive-trek to the sacred Mount Kailas and Manasarovar Lake requires at least 24 days and lots of endurance. The trek itself is a religious circumambulation of the revered peak but it takes many days of driving and camping to get there.

Mountain Biking in Tibet

Hardy travellers can now mountain bike through Tibet. Kathmandu's Himalayan Mountain Bikes offers three summer itineraries and provides all bicycles, helmets, equipment, food and support services.

All trips begin with a week's stay in Kathmandu while visas and other travel documents are secured for the expedition. Aside from useful orientation sessions, you are at leisure to explore Kathmandu Valley. For details, contact **Himalayan Mountain Bikes**, P.O. Box 2247, Kathmandu, Nepal (tel: and fax: 977-1-411724).

Lhasa to Kathmandu
15 days

Fly to Lhasa and spend a day and a half exploring the city and acclimatising yourself. With stops for sightseeing, accommodation in hotels where they exist or otherwise camping, you bike via Shigatse and cross into Nepal on Day 15. You are met across the border and driven to Kathmandu.

Lhasa, Gyantse, Yarlung Valley
12 days

Fly from Kathmandu and spend 3 days exploring Lhasa. On Day 4, ride for 3 days along the paved northern road, turning south on a gravel road to Gyantse (Gyantze) which you explore. For 2 days, head into the remote hills to the southeast, passing north of the huge Yamdrok Tsho lake and on Day 9 down the Kamba La mountain. On Day 10, bike to Tsetang (Zetang), spending the following day exploring the Yarlung Valley. On Day 12 you are driven to Gongkar Airport.

Tsetang, Gyantse and Lhasa
8 days

Fly from Kathmandu to Gongkar Airport and drive to Tsetang. The next 2 days include a bike ride east to the castle at Yumbu Lagang and to the Valley of the Kings at Chongye. On Day 4, drive and bike to Mindroling, and on Day 5, to Chushul. On Day 6, bike into Lhasa, spending the following day exploring. On Day 8, transfer to the airport.

Everest from Rongbuk (Dza Rongphu) Monastery

Shopping

Shopping is somewhat limited in Lhasa and more so in the small towns of Central Tibet. Prices are generally lower in Shigatse (Xigaze) and Gyantse (Gyantze) than at Lhasa. You'll find a wider range, better quality and lower prices in Kathmandu but the shopping is not as fun and you will not find a more jovial bunch of bargainers than in Tibet.

Silver, gold, turquoise and coral are the raw materials for a wide array of jewellery items that resemble those made by the Navajo of the American Southwest. Most popular are necklaces made of turquoise and coral; tiny silver (often combined with burl wood) snuff bottles; small Buddhist amulets in filigree silver studded with turquoise and coral; herders' knives and more elaborate swords, both encased in carved silver sheathes; shiny silver boxes bejewelled with turquoise; brass and copper teapots; yak butter tea churns; silver-lined bowls for drinking tea; engraved silver or metal butter lamps; handsomely decorated flint and steel sets normally worn on a nomad's belt; flat spoons and brass ladles and other kitchen utensils.

Tibetans are born traders

Other items include Tibetan fur-lined hats decorated with brocade flowers in silver and gold threads, brocade and silver belts, painted *thangkas* and metal cymbals. Some items are old but most have been recently produced for the tourist market and the workmanship shows it. It is rare that you will find a genuine piece of art but if you do, it may have been stolen from a monastery and is bound to be confiscated by customs upon departure.

Brass prayer wheels

Lobbies of major hotels in Lhasa, Gyantse and Shigatse carry items not normally found in the local markets. Tibetan costumes and masks at fixed prices are among the many items offered. Lhasa also has several art galleries. The Tibet Art Gallery on Dekyi Shar Lam at the foot of the Potala Palace offers paintings in a variety of styles and subjects.

The Lhasa Carpet Factory near the Tibetan University and the Shigatse Carpet Factory in front of the Tashilhunpo Monastery use ancient techniques and modern dyes to handweave handsome carpets with traditional designs. Be aware that better quality carpets, and a wider choice too, are produced in Kathmandu.

Of the provincial towns, Shigatse's free market offers shopping opportunities that are on a par with Lhasa. Gyantse's free market is good for practical items like horse bridles and stirrups, butter churns, traditional door locks and ornately-painted wooden chests, but the selection is limited. In the main streets around Tsetang, Gyantse and Shigatse, look for vendors who sell brightly-coloured Qinghai carpets.

Eating Out

'**D**ining' may not be the correct term for mealtimes in Tibet: 'refueling' might be more apt. Tibetans consume a spartan diet that provides them with energy and heat to get through the cold days. Vegetables are seasonal and selection is limited. Thus, Tibetan cuisine tends towards *tsampa*, a flour ground from roasted highland barley, meats, oils and peppery spices.

It is quickly apparent that the diet has not stunted the Tibetans. Many men are as tall as Europeans. Nor do they become bulky as do Eskimos, Italians and native Americans who thrive on similar diets. But the diet is slowly changing as road improvements allow for the importation of foodstuffs from the east and as the Chinese preference for vegetables influences the eating habits of Tibetans.

In major Lhasa hotels, European or Chinese meals are almost on par with those in other Asian cities. In other Tibetan towns, hotel restaurants sometimes offer a choice between Tibetan, Chinese and European fare. European breakfasts for instance include eggs, semi-sweet cakes and coffee. Chinese breakfasts usually feature *congee* (a thin rice gruel), roasted peanuts, pickled vegetables, dumplings and green tea.

Tibetan Food

Dried mutton and Tibetan tea

At banquets, a Tibetan dinner begins with cold appetizers, followed by a main course of several hot dishes. Meats are generally boiled to tenderise them and then stir-fried with other ingredients. An important mainstay of the Tibetan diet is *tsampa*, a barley flour mixed with tea and butter or eaten dry. Main dishes are usually accompanied by noodles or dumplings as good rice is scarce. Soup with a meat base is usually an integral part of the meal, especially if *momos*, steamed meat dumplings like giant ravioli, are served. Fried *momos*, called *kothay* are particularly tasty.

Another favourite of mine is *shabalay*, deep-fried meat pies which are served with a spicy salad made from radish or cabbage, rather

Multi-lingual signboard

like Korean *kimchi*. Tibetans like hot chillies with their meat dishes but these are usually served separately or sliced and dunked in a vinegar sauce.

Meat is very popular in Tibet and non-Buddhists are employed to kill the animals. Dried yak meat is especially good for travelling in these cold climes, as is another unusual snack – a hard cheese made of yak milk and sucked like a boiled sweet. Tibetans generally do not follow the meal with dessert. In many restaurants, diners eat with chopsticks. In the rural areas, people eat with spoons or directly from their bowls without utensils.

Drinks

The drink which you will become most familiar with by the end of your stay is jasmine tea. For contrast, try the unique Tibetan yak-butter tea. To make it, tea leaves are boiled and pounded in a churn with yak butter and salt. This tea is then kept hot in a thermos for use during the day. Never drink it cold: the globules of congealed fat that float to the surface are less than appetising, and cold tea may lead to tummy upsets. You will be better equipped to handle the unusual taste of Tibetan tea if you think of it as a soup.

Most hotel bars serve alcoholic drinks using spirits distilled in China; in Lhasa, imported liquors are also available. Chinese wines are usually sweet. Lhasa Beer is the most popular light beer available. Tibetan beer, known as *chang*, is made from fermented barley and occasionally, rice or millet. It tastes mild but is seldom made with pure water and can sneak up on you after a few glasses, having an especially strong effect at Tibet's high altitudes. The Changs Bar in the Holiday Inn Lhasa serves a delicious *chang* drink laced with honey.

Yak butter tea

Restaurants

Bold diners will find eating adventures waiting near their hotels. The interiors of these restaurants may look scruffy, the lighting may be dim, and the air filled with acrid smoke but Western gourmets shell out lots of money for similar atmosphere in restaurants back home. Here, it is for practically nothing.

Sanitation standards at these places are not the highest but independent travellers have been dining in these places for years and have survived. As a general rule, if the food is freshly cooked, it's reasonably safe to consume.

The **Gang Gyen Sakang** at Dekyi Shar Lam (tel: 25327) serves tasty Tibetan food. If you have a party of diners, the Tibetan women owners may even serenade you with Tibetan love songs. The restaurant is open daily 11am–11pm. The **Crazy Yak Saloon and Restaurant** on Dekyi Shar Lam, next to the Yak Hotel entrance, offers Tibetan and Chinese food in a comfortable atmosphere with overstuffed leather chairs to relax in. Tibetan banquets can be arranged for groups.

A firm favourite with travellers is the **Kailash Restaurant** in the Banok Shol Hotel (tel: 23829) on Dekyi Shar Lam which serves a variety of Tibetan, Chinese and Western dishes, including spaghetti and lasagne. Just off Dekyi Shar Lam is a nameless Tibetan eatery dubbed **The Pink Curtain**, thanks to the pink curtain hanging over its doorway. Like most Tibetan eateries, the menu is loaded with mostly meat dishes; try the roast lamb and fried potatoes. **Tashi's Restaurant** 1 and 2 on Dekyi Shar Lam serves inexpensive yet delicious Tibetan and Western food, including cheese cake.

Restaurant sign

If you're not very hungry, the **Barkhor Cafe** on the upper terrace, southwest corner of the Barkhor Square, is perfect for light lunches and beverages. Operated by Holiday Inn Lhasa, its open terrace is a good place to watch the passing crowd. **Fu Rong Restaurant**, on the right, a short way down Dekyi Nub Lam from the Holiday Inn Lhasa, serves Szechuan dishes with noodles or rice.

Muslim restaurants are scattered throughout Lhasa, particularly on or near Dekyi Shar Lam and near the Barkor. Look for long green banners hanging outside of restaurants with the Muslim moon and star symbol in white. The staff typically wear white caps. The restaurants offer inexpensive but delicious noodle dishes, and the meat used is lamb rather than pork. Try *gan-ba* which is like spaghetti with meat sauce, and *mien tau*, a hearty noodle and lamb soup.

Gyantse and Shigatse

The farther west you go in Tibet, the fewer opportunities there are for dining outside the hotel. The fare in rural Tibetan restaurants is very basic; a basket of boiled mutton legs or shanks and a sharp knife arrive at the table and you slice off whatever you want.

To the left of the Gyantse Hotel gate in **Gyantse** are several Muslim restaurants. Identified by the blue banners with white Chinese characters, they serve bowls of broth with chunks of yak and sheep meat and dumplings. To the right of the Xigatse Hotel in **Shigatse** are several small Chinese restaurants serving basic cuisine. Several good Muslim restaurants are found across the Tibetan market.

Calendar of Special Events

Luck or careful planning will put you in Tibet during one of these festivals. As their dates are linked to the Tibetan lunar calendar or are calculated by astrologers, dates vary each year and can be difficult to determine in advance.

JANUARY – MARCH

Tibetan New Year (Losar), nationwide, February/March: Tibet's most important festival officially takes place over 3 days but traditionally lasts for nearly 2 weeks. It is marked with family celebrations, dramas and carnivals, horse races, archery competitions, picnicking and much drinking of *chang*. Pilgrims also make incense offerings on the hills around Lhasa.

During the final days of the Tibetan Year, monks craft beautiful butter and *tsampa* (barley flour) sculptures called *torma*. These depict religious scenes and deities and are displayed in chapels where they will remain until the following Losar.

Great Prayer Festival (Monlam Chenmo), Lhasa, February/March: Just after the Tibetan New Year, this auspicious festival was held annually until it was suspended in 1959. Monks used to travel from Drepung, Sera and Ganden monasteries to Lhasa's

A festive wall hanging

Jokhang temple to chant, listen to a sermon by the Dalai Lama and to debate on religious doctrine. Many monks sat for examinations to earn higher degrees. This festival may be revived in the near future.

Butter Sculpture Festival (Chonga Chopa), Lhasa, February/March: Celebrated as part of the Great Prayer Festival, the highlight is the Jokhang temple's display of huge, intricately carved butter sculptures on the 15th day of the first Tibetan month.

Thousands of butter lamps are lit inside and outside the Jokhang giving it a very festive atmosphere, and laymen pass through to pay their respects to the Buddha.

Butter sculptures

Gyantse horse festival

MAY – JULY

Buddha's Birthday (Saga Dawa), nationwide, May/June: In memory of Buddha Sakyamuni's birth and enlightenment, Tibetan pilgrims carry offerings of food and money to monasteries throughout the fourth Tibetan month. Captured animals are set free and thousands of pilgrims and monks throng the Jokhang Temple.

Gyantse Horse Racing and Archery (Gyantse Damang), Gyantse, May/June: Tibetans are known for their excellent horsemanship. This festival celebrates their marksmanship while riding at full tilt. On the first day, monks perform a masked dance in the Kumbum Stupa courtyard. On the succeeding 4 days, Tibetans erect tents and enjoy picnics amidst much revelry. Among the competitions is one where horsemen galloping at full speed lean down to snatch *katas* (ceremonial scarfs) which have been placed at intervals along the ground. Horse-

borne archers also shoot arrows at stationary targets.

Samye Cham Festival, Samye, June/July: Both pilgrims and monks from distant monasteries journey to Samye to watch masked dances and obtain the blessings of the Buddha who descends to earth bringing eternal peace and happiness.

The Universal Incense Offering Festival (Dzamling Chisang), nationwide, June/July: This special day is dedicated to praying for peace in the world. Pilgrims carry money and incense to temples and climb holy mountains – notably Gambay Utse, behind Drepung Monastery and Chaksamchari, near the Chushul Bridge, on the way to the airport.

Ganden Thangka Festival (Ganden Khi-khu), Ganden Monastery, July: Ganden's monks hang an enormous *thangka* from the special wall at the northern corner of the monastery where it can be seen from the surrounding countryside. Chanting prayers to the accompaniment of the long copper and brass horns (*tongchen*), they honour the founder of the Gelugpa sect.

The Fourth of the Sixth Month Festival (Drukpa Tse Shi), Lhasa and Shigatse, July/August: The name refers to the fourth day of the sixth month of the Tibetan calendar when, long ago, Buddha is said to have come down to earth to help people.

The day honours both his selflessness and expresses the hope that he will return one day. In Lhasa, many Buddhists make a holy lingkor circuit, burning fragrant incense along the way.

Yoghurt festival costume

87

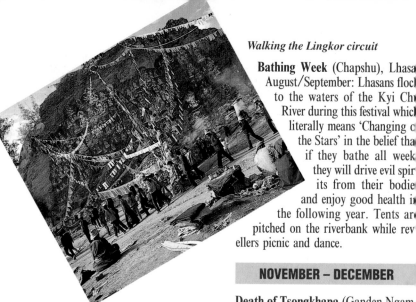
Walking the Lingkor circuit

Bathing Week (Chapshu), Lhasa, August/September: Lhasans flock to the waters of the Kyi Chu River during this festival which literally means 'Changing of the Stars' in the belief that if they bathe all week they will drive evil spirits from their bodies and enjoy good health in the following year. Tents are pitched on the riverbank while revellers picnic and dance.

NOVEMBER – DECEMBER

Death of Tsongkhapa (Ganden Ngamchu), nationwide, November/December: In the memory of Tsongkhapa, Buddhists say morning prayers at the monasteries on the 24th and 25th day of the 10th Tibetan month. Walk around the Barkor circuit and join the thousands of pilgrims who come to Lhasa every winter on pilgrimage from the far corners of Tibet.

In the evening, Tibetans eat a special kind of *thukpa* which represents sadness. Monks illuminate the exteriors of their monasteries, and families place lighted yak butter lamps on the window sills or roofs of their houses.

AUGUST – SEPTEMBER

Yoghurt Festival (Shodun) or the **Tibetan Opera Festival**, Lhasa, August/September: Celebrated at Drepung and in Sera, the festival begins at dawn when monks hang a huge *thangka* from the monastery wall for all to see. The highlight occurs when monks perform a masked dance, a form of opera, to drive away evil spirits.

Traditionally, Lhasa residents picnic in Lukhang Lake park behind the Potala, or pitch tents in the Norbulingka gardens, the main venue for a week of daily performances by opera troupes from all over the country.

Damshung Horse Races, Damshung (near Lake Nam Tsho, 170km/106 miles north of Lhasa), August/September: A one-week horse racing and archery competition similar to that held at Gyantse.

Nagchu Horse Races, Nagchu (330km/205 miles west of Lhasa), August/September: Lasting one week, it is celebrated in a manner similar to that of the Gyantse horse racing and archery celebration.

Masked dancers

PRACTICAL information

GETTING THERE

By Air and Road

Visitors generally fly in to Lhasa from Chengdu in southwest China, or Kathmandu. You can also drive from Lhasa to Kathmandu in 2–3 days non-stop. Most travellers prefer to make it a more leisurely 4- or 5-night adventure to enjoy the sites en route. The most popular tours last for 1–2 weeks; flying in to Lhasa and touring the sites of Lhasa and the Yarlung Valley and then embarking on the spectacular overland drive across Central Tibet to Zhangmu and the Nepalese border at Kodari. The trip can also be done in reverse, ie starting from Kathmandu and ending in Lhasa though it is not so good for acclimatisation. There are a number of fly and drive combinations of varying lengths. More ambitious tours combine city sightseeing with several weeks of trekking in Tibet, often involving long and spectacular drives.

China Southwest Airlines (CSWA), the regional arm of the national airline, CAAC, serves Lhasa with two daily flights from Chengdu at 6.50am and 7am, arriving at 8.50am and 9am respectively. Return flights depart Lhasa at 9.40am and 9.50am, arriving in Chengdu at 11.25am and 11.35am. Several charter flights connect Chengdu and Hong Kong every week and there are daily connections with Beijing via Chengdu.

On Tuesday and Saturday, CSWA's spectacular flight from Kathmandu to Lhasa across the Himalaya, departs Kathmandu at 10am, arriving in Lhasa at 1pm. The return flight departs Lhasa on Saturday at 10am, arriving in Kathmandu at 8.45am.

Distances Between Key Towns

Lhasa-Gongkar airport 93km (58 miles)
Gongkar-Tsetang (Zetang) 97km (60 miles)
Gongkar-Chushul Bridge 25km (16 miles)
Chushul Bridge-Gyantse (Gyantze) 193km (120 miles)
Gyantse-Shigatse (Xigaze) 90km (56 miles)
Shigatse-Shegar (Xegar) 239km (149 miles)
Shegar-Zhangmu 251km (156 miles)
Zhangmu-Kodari 8km (5 miles)
Kodari-Kathmandu 114km (71 miles)

Airport Tax

There is an airport departure tax of 60 yuan for international flights to Kathmandu, and 30 yuan for domestic flights.

TRAVEL ESSENTIALS

When to Visit

The best period is March to October when the days are not too cold and the passes are clear of snow. The weather is generally arid with temperatures ranging from be-

Embarking for Tibet

low freezing in winter to hot in summer. The winter season is from November to mid-March, the rainy season from mid-June to early September and autumn is from September to October. February, March and June–September are the best months for festivals. During the June–September monsoon season, landslides can delay journeys through the mountains to Nepal. From November through February, some of Tibet's most interesting migratory birds fly in.

Visas and Permits

The only travel permitted to Tibet is in organised groups. These can be booked either with a travel operator at home who deals directly with Lhasa or more usually through specially approved Kathmandu- or Hong Kong-based travel agencies. Only when you book a tour is the Tibet visa issued. This is not as limiting as it sounds as a one-person 'group' can easily be arranged although it is more expensive to do so. Trips range from 'budget' travel by bus and accommodation in simple hotels to 'luxurious' tours in private cars. Listed on page 99 are travel agents who specialise in Tibet. When you book a tour with them, the Tibet visa will be issued on receipt of clearance from Beijing. The visa can be sent for collection to a Chinese embassy of your choice. Allow for delays. If travelling via Kathmandu, it is advisable to let your agent collect the Tibet visa. The visa form requires two passport photos, a fee of between US$12 and US$32 and 3 days to process. A 1-day express service is available for an additional fee.

On arrival in Tibet, your Lhasa agent will give you a Government Travel Permit valid for Lhasa, and an Alien Travel Permit to travel to cities outside of Lhasa. These are measures designed to curtail individual travellers who still sometimes contrive to travel on their own.

Visas for Nepal: The Royal Nepal Embassy (open Monday to Friday 9.30am–12.30pm, tel: 22880) in Gyatso Tou Lam, opposite the north wall of the Norbulingka Palace in Lhasa, issues 30-day visas in 24 hours on presentation of your passport, one photo and 250 yuan. A 30-day visa can also be obtained at the Nepalese border checkpost at Kodari for US$25 and one passport photo. It is best is to obtain a double entry Nepal visa from the Royal Nepal Embassy closest to your home before you start your journey.

Customs

There is no prohibition on bringing still and video cameras, tape recorders or radios as long as they are registered with a Customs official. Permits to make commercial films in Tibet must be obtained in advance. Printed matter deemed unsuitable by the Chinese government are prohibited. At the moment, photographs of the Dalai Lama are permitted as long as they do not contain Tibetan script or the Tibetan flag. Political situations change, however, and to secure them from possible confiscation, store them out of sight.

Note that Chinese law prohibits the export of items made before 1959. Customs officials will ask for receipts for questionable items, but are generally lenient for all but obvious antiques.

Customs regulations forbid the export of souvenirs in amounts deemed to be excessive. Except for carpets shipped by the Shigatse and Lhasa carpet factories, it is safer to carry your souvenir items with you and pay excess baggage charges, if any.

Vaccinations

There is no smallpox or malaria in Tibet and the cholera vaccine is not necessary. Check that your inoculations are up to date for typhoid, tetanus and diphtheria. Gamma Globulin against Hepatitis A is strongly advised.

What to Bring

Clothing: Dress for warmth and in layers as there are considerable temperature differences between dawn and noon, sun and shade. With dripping butter in every monastery and dust blowing across every road, dark-coloured clothes are advised.

From October to April, a down jacket is essential, even if only for sitting in Tibet's unheated hotel rooms. Trekking shops in Kathmandu's Thamel district rent them for less than a dollar per day but insist on a US$50 deposit or a credit card imprint. Down pants, also for rent in Kathmandu, are recommended during the winter months. Jogging shoes with treads are advised, especially in monasteries with stairs that are clad in slippery steel plates. In the winter, insert Dr Scholl's or similar thermal liners in your shoes to insulate against cold from the ground.

Bring heavy socks, a balaclava and a scarf to protect your face against dust. Take mittens for early morning bicycle rides. As the Tibetan sun is very bright, sunglasses and a hat are essential.

Toiletries: Sunscreen, toilet paper – toilet facilities are primitive, no toilet paper and wash basins except in hotels – lots of moisturising lotion and lip balm are essential. Many travellers recommend surgical face masks against the fine dust but if you are riding in a closed vehicle, a cotton scarf will probably be more useful. Masks can be purchased at pharmacies in Lhasa or Kathmandu.

Other Useful Items: A canteen, cup and spoon (usually not included in packed lunches), a strong flashlight to see monastery murals, a knife with a can opener, a thin rope laundry line, and cold water detergent to wash small items. A star map is useful for the dazzlingly clear nights. During the summer months, you may need a raincoat or umbrella.

Food Bag: Meals may pose a problem if you are accustomed only to Western food. While hotel food is generally quite good and quantities are sufficient, consider carrying snacks with you. Some suggestions: packet soups, instant coffee and powdered drinks as hot water is usually available, nuts, candy, cheese, dried fruit, chocolate, peanut butter, jam, crackers, muesli, tuna fish and sardines.

What to Wear

The number of tourists who think they are in Palm Beach and walk about in shorts, sandals, or are braless in loose T-shirts is surprising. A quick look around will suggest that even in summer, Tibetans cover most of their bodies, not just to keep warm, but also to maintain decorum. Respect their culture by showing a little mature consideration, particularly when visiting monasteries. Loose-fitting pants or skirts for women and long pants for men will meet the dress requirements; shorts are not appropriate at any time.

Time Zones and Electricity

Tibet is 8 hours ahead of GMT. Note: Tibet is linked to Beijing time so when you cross the border to Nepal the time change is considerable. Nepal is 5 hours and 45 minutes ahead of GMT. The standard voltage in Tibet is 220 volts.

GETTING ACQUAINTED

Geography

The Tibet Autonomous Region measures 2,600km (1,625 miles) from east to west and 1,300km (812 miles) north to south for a total area of 1,221,700sq km (471,900sq miles), or roughly the area of Peru. While the average elevation is 5,000m (16,500ft), most of the populated areas lie between 3,500 and 4,000m (11,500–13,100ft) elevation.

Bordered by Nepal, Bhutan and India, Tibet boasts four of the world's highest mountains: Mount Everest at 8,848m (29,028ft), shares a common frontier with Nepal; Cho Oyu; Makalu; and Shishapangma, the world's 14th highest peak and entirely in Tibet.

The populated central portion of Tibet lies in the rain shadow of the Himalaya, giving it an arid climate that supports very limited vegetation. Its southeastern quadrant is covered in forests, making it China's second largest source of timber.

According to a 1993 Chinese census, the Tibet Autonomous Region's population numbered 2.29 million. With its previous wider boundaries, the Tibetan population is now more than double that figure. Lhasa, the capital, is estimated to hold between 300,000 to 400,000 people.

Government

Before 1950, Tibet was an independent country governed by the Dalai Lama and hierarchs of the Gelugpa sect, as well as by members of elite noble families. Following the capture of East Tibet by Communist China in 1950, the Tibetan government agreed to signing the 17-Point Agreement, which gave Tibet control over its domestic and religious affairs, but gave the Chinese control over Tibet's external and international affairs, as well as allowing the Chinese army to advance 'peacefully' into Lhasa. In March 1959, relations in Lhasa between China and Tibet soured, the Dalai Lama secretly fled to India, and a popular Tibetan uprising against the Chinese was crushed. Since then, the Chinese central government has ruled Tibet. The Dalai Lama has remained in India and continues to head the Tibetan Government-in-Exile, based in Dharamsala, with hopes of returning to Tibet one day. In 1965, China declared Tibet as the Tibet Autonomous Region (TAR), which in theory meant that Tibet would have autonomy over its internal affairs. In reality, Tibet continues to be ruled directly from Beijing, with hundreds of thousands of soldiers stationed throughout the countryside and in Lhasa. Today, Tibet still waits for one of her own people to be appointed as leader of their 'autonomous' region.

Economy

The traditional economy of Tibet was based on agriculture and pastoralism, with the majority of the population involved in these livelihoods during the summer months. In winter, male members of households would move about the country, engaging in trading activities. During the 1960s and 70s, much of this system was dismantled by the Chinese government, though economic reforms introduced since the early 1980s have encouraged many of the traditional practices of farming and herding to return. Traders, however, do not have the same freedom to roam as they once did. Farmers and herders are still required to sell certain amounts of their goods to the government at low, fixed prices, although they are now allowed to sell their surplus at the actual market rates.

Tourism is the main foreign income earner for Tibet, though Chinese plans to modernize Tibet over the next decade are targeting development in agriculture, light industries and mining. At press time, almost all manufactured goods, all motor fuel and much of the food consumed by the Chinese in Tibet must be imported by truck from mainland China. A controversial hydro-electric power plant was constructed on Lake Yamdrok Tsho to provide electricity for the various development plans. New paved roads have been completed between the agricultural heartlands of Central Tibet, from Lhasa to Shigatse and Tsetang, and older buildings in Lhasa are being torn down to provide housing for the influx of skilled Chinese workers and economic migrants expected to settle in Tibet from the Chinese mainland.

How Not to Offend

As with anywhere in the world, taking time to learn a few simple words of Tibetan will please those you meet.

In monasteries and homes, Tibetan hospitality is such that you will be offered endless refills of yak butter tea when you've barely taken two sips of the previous cup. To avoid bladder distension or giving offense to your hosts, begin protesting gently (smiling broadly) that you are full long before you really are. When the tea is poured for you, hold the cup with both hands (or touch the sides with your fingertips) as a gesture of appreciation for what you are receiving from your hosts.

When visiting monasteries, hats but not shoes have to be removed at the door. Walk clockwise around the prayer hall and outdoors keep *stupas*, shrines and prayer wheels on your right shoulder as a mark of respect.

Monks are required by Chinese regulation to charge foreigners for taking photographs inside their monasteries. In general, a single fee covers any number of shots you may wish to take in any number of chapels. Sometimes you may be charged a fee for a single chapel.

Sky burial sites where Tibetans dispose of their dead to vultures are usually located on hills near monasteries but these are strictly off-limits to foreigners.

Culture

Women in Tibet: Traditionally, women in Tibet were not subservient to men in rank but owned land and conducted businesses with equal status. Tibetan society, until recently, practised polyandry, whereby a woman may be married to two or even three men simultaneously, usually brothers. This was economically expedient in remote villages for security and to keep precious cultivated land from being divided.

Nuns (*anis*) are, however, regarded as inferior to monks. Be aware that there are chapels in some Tibetan monasteries which are off-limits to women because the spirits might be offended.

Tibetan Names: Only in rare instances do Tibetans use surnames; normally they use single or double first names. Names for men are given by lamas, including a middle name which gives the person his individuality. Many Tibetan names have beautiful meanings.

Photos of the Dalai Lama: It is not encouraged to carry photos of the Dalai Lama into Tibet and your baggage will be searched on arrival. Checks are cursory though. One area in which you will have to make your own decision regards pleas for photos of the Dalai Lama.

Many of the requests are arbitrary and the supplicants may already have several portraits on their altars. Moreover, giving to one person can cause a stampede. Tibetologist Gary McCue suggests that they be given out selectively, not to those who merely request them, but to those who have performed small services.

Beggars: There are two types of people seeking alms: pilgrims and beggars. Donating up to 2 jiao to pilgrims will earn you blessings. On the other hand, beggars, many of them Chinese, are professionals; donate a few small bills if you wish, particularly if they are handicapped.

Language

Despite its proximity to Asia's two largest civilisations, the Tibetan language bears little resemblance to those of India or China. It falls into a category called Tibeto-Burman although Tibet shares few cultural traits with the Hinayana Buddhist culture of its Southeast Asian neighbour. Based on a form of Sanskrit derived from India in the 7th century, the Tibetan alphabet comprises 30 letters.

MONEY MATTERS

Currency

China has abandoned its dual currency system for a single currency. All prices are now in the official renmimbi yuan (RMB). Chinese currency is counted in yuan, jiao (also known as mao) and fen. One yuan is divided into 100 fen or 10 jiao; 1 jiao is equivalent to 10 fen. Bills are denominated in 1, 2 and 5 fen notes, 1, 2 and 5 jiao notes, and 1, 2, 5, 10, 50 and 100 yuan notes.

At the time of press, the exchange rate was about 10 yuan to one US dollar. Money can be changed only at the Bank of China (branches in Lhasa, Shigatse and Zhangmu) or at major hotels. Hotels charge a 1.5 percent commission.

Credit Cards

American Express, Visa, Great Wall and other credit cards are accepted at the Lhasa Holiday Inn, the Tibet Hotel and the Bank of China main branch.

Tipping

There is no policy of tipping of hotel staff, porters or waiters. You may wish to give some cigarettes to your guide and driver – '555' is the preferred foreign brand (available at Kathmandu airport). At the end of the trip, consider tipping the driver and guide for good services. Small gifts are much appreciated.

GETTING AROUND

Landcruiser

If you are on a tour, you will travel in a landcruiser or mini-van. Local travel companies in Lhasa rent Toyota landcruisers for 3.5 yuan per kilometre. For trips of more than 1 day, you pay a surcharge of 450 yuan per night.

Bus

Minibuses run between Lhasa and Sera, and Lhasa and Drepung. Find them on Mi Mang Lam or along Dekyi Shar Lam.

Buses leave from the New Bus Station in Lhasa for Tsetang, Shigatse and Zhangmu daily, and Golmud three times a month. Reaching Samye, Sakya and other sites located between big towns is easy; getting back is difficult. You may have to flag down whatever will stop – truck, jeep, donkey cart, yak – to get home.

Buses travel from Shigatse to Sakya on Tuesday and Saturday, with the return journey to Shigatse on Wednesday and Sunday.

Bicycle

To travel around Lhasa on your own, rent a bicycle or take a rickshaw. Other Tibetan cities lack public transportation but are so small that a 10-minute walk will get you almost anywhere you want to go. Rent bicycles from the Snowland, Yak, Kirey or Banak Shol hotels for 10 yuan per day; non-guests must leave their passports or a 200-yuan deposit.

HOURS AND HOLIDAYS

Business Hours

Government offices and banks are open from 10am–1pm and 3.30–7pm in winter; 9.30am–12.30pm and 4–7.30pm in summer. Shops operate from 10am–7pm in winter; 9.30am–8pm in summer.

Public Holidays

There are 13 public holidays a year in Tibet. Sunday is the official day off.
January 1: New Year's Day; 2 days.
February*: Chinese Spring Festival; 3 days.
Feb/Mar*: Tibetan New Year; 3 days.
May 1: Labour Day
May 4: Youth Day
June 1: Children's Day
August 1: Army Day
August*: Yoghurt Festival
* Dates subject to the lunar calendar

ACCOMMODATION

Apart from the international-class Holiday Inn in Lhasa, you will find two types of accommodation available: Chinese and Tibetan. In both, facilities are very basic. Tour groups are usually accommodated in Chinese hotels. Most hotels in Lhasa have restaurants and most rooms are equipped with televisions and hot water. Outside Lhasa, few hotel rooms have hot water or are heated, although thick quilts will keep you warm. Tibetan-style hotels are just as spartan but many, surprisingly, have heaters in the rooms. Doubles and rooms with as many as 8 beds are the norm and they are usually more centrally located than Chinese hotels. Standard double room rates are categorized as follows: $$$=350 yuan and above; $$=100–350 yuan; $=100 yuan and below

Lhasa

HOLIDAY INN LHASA
1 Minzu Road
Tel: 32221
Fax: 35796
The only international-class hotel in town. 450 heated rooms with television. Four restaurants, bar, gift shop, in-house movies, beauty salon and swimming pool. $$$

TIBET HOTEL
Dekyi Nub Lam
Tel: 33738
Large and popular with Asian tourists.
96 rooms. Good facilities. $$$

SUNLIGHT HOTEL
Linju Road
Tel: 22431
Located at the eastern end of the city near
Tibet University. $$

SNOWLAND HOTEL
Mentsi Khang Road
Tel: 23687
Communal baths with hot water. 30
rooms. Good location near Jokhang.
Pleasant Tibetan staff. $

YAK HOTEL
Dekyi Shar Lam
Tel: 23496
Communal baths with hot water. Centrally
located near major attractions. Friendly
Tibetan staff. $–$$

BANAK SHOL
Dekyi Shar Lam
Tel: 23829
Communal baths with hot water. Tibetan-
run hotel. $

Tsetang (Zetang)

ZE DONG HOTEL
Chinese-style hotel. Hot water after 8pm
only. Rooms are not heated. Chinese
restaurant. Located on the southern edge
of town. $$

HIMALAYAN TIBETAN HOTEL
Tibetan-style hotel. Centre of town near
the traffic roundabout. $

Gyantse (Gyantze)

GYANGTSE HOTEL
Located at the southern end of town. Has
both Chinese-style and Tibetan-style rooms.
Hot water, but no heater. $$

GYANTSE HOTEL
A no-frills Tibetan-style hotel located at
the main street near the Gyantse Dzong.
$

Shigatse (Xigaze)

XIGAZE HOTEL
Chinese-run hotel. Rooms are not heated
and hot water is available only after 9pm.
Chinese restaurant. $$

TIBETAN TENZIN HOTEL
Located opposite the Tibetan free mar-
ket, this Tibetan-style hotel has 20 rooms.
Communal bathrooms with cold water
shower. Charcoal heaters to keep you
warm. $

Shegar (Xegar)

SHEGAR GUEST HOUSE
Located at the southern edge of town.
Tibetan-style with barracks-like accom-
modation. No heaters, no hot water. The
coldest night you'll spend in Tibet. Climb
up the iron rungs to the roof for a breath-
taking view of the night sky $

QOMOLANGMA
On the main highway at the junction with
the road to Shegar. Hot water, no heaters.
Better facilities but far from Shegar $$

Zhangmu (Khasa)

ZHANGMU HOTEL
Chinese-style hotel along the main road.
No hot water, no heater. Only rooms on
third and fourth floors have attached baths
and balconies with beautiful views of the
town. $$

General Health
Tibet's thin air and dust pose consider-
able medical problems if you are not in the
best of health. In addition, the lack of

medical facilities, doctors who speak little or no English, and the difficulties involved in evacuating a sick person do not recommend it to someone who is not fit. If you have heart or respiratory problems, ask your doctor about the advisability of a Tibet trip. Tell him of the altitude (3,500–5,300m/11,400–17,400ft) the dry, dusty air, and the need to climb steep stairs.

Hygiene

As you do not want to spoil your visit with illness, the most obvious course of action is prevention. Drink only bottled drinks, freshly-boiled water from your hotel, and tea. Carry a canteen while on the road and disinfect your own drinking water with tablets such as Puritabs. You cannot drink enough liquids in Tibet. The air and your rapid breathing dries you out faster than you think. A large intake of liquid significantly helps your body acclimatise to the high altitudes.

Food sanitation in the large hotels is generally good but with small restaurants or street vendors the general rule is to be cautious: Boil it, peel it or forget it. Avoid any cold food and vegetable salads.

Medical Problems

Dr David R Shlim, Medical Director of the Himalayan Rescue Association and the well-regarded CIWEC clinic in Kathmandu, warns of potential problems in Tibet. Germs on the whole do not thrive in these cold conditions. While there are many types of stomach disorders, few constitute major health threats.

The most common complaints in Tibet are respiratory in nature. Coughs are caused by the dry air, often laden with smoke or dust. Leave your contact lenses at home and wear glasses instead.

Tibet's dry climate takes a toll on skin. Apply moisturising cream liberally and carry lip balm to prevent chapped lips.

Diarrhoea: Medicines are available in Kathmandu without prescription. The following is a guideline but it is always best to have a stool test and seek medical ad-

vice if you can. A general exam at the journey's end is advised.

The most common diarrhoea is a bacterial infection and the onset is rapid. If you have to make a run for the bathroom, you are likely to have bacterial diarrhoea. Begin antibiotic treatment as soon as you have stopped vomiting. One tablet of Norfloxacin or Ciprofloxacin in the morning and one in the evening for 3 days is best. Drink plenty of liquids. Less common is giardia whose telltale symptoms include mild intestinal cramping, foul-tasting burps and flatulence. It is generally more annoying than painful and may subside for a day or two before reappearing. Giardia often does not show up in stool exams. Treating yourself with a one-time, 2g (four 500mg tablets) dose of tinidazole (brand name, Tiniba) is 95 percent effective. Take the medicine at night and do not drink alcohol.

Amoebic dysentery is more rare and can only be detected with a stool exam. Symptoms include abdominal pain, diarrhoea (occasionally alternating with constipation) and sometimes blood in the stool. The most telling symptoms are weight-loss and chronic fatigue. Seek medical advice.

Hepatitis A: Gamma Globulin is considered effective in preventing the disease; watching what you eat is also wise.

Nepal has the most cases of Hepatitis A in the summer months when you are most likely to be visiting. However, you are unlikely to contract other types of hepatitis in Tibet.

Rabies: Tibetan dogs can be fierce and the disease is endemic. If you are bitten, it is wise to assume the dog has rabies and take the necessary injections as soon as you can. Unless you are on a long trek in Tibet, you will have time to get to Kathmandu, Hong Kong or home for treatment.

Acute Mountain Sickness (AMS): High altitude can affect all travellers in various ways that have little to do with the sufferer's age, sex or physical fitness. There is no way to predict how you will react but if you have a history of heart or respiratory problems, consult your physician.

Over 2,800m (9,000ft), do not exert yourself or push yourself too fast; drink plenty of liquids and watch for warning signs. Keep activity to a minimum for the first day. If you feel tired, rest. You may be travelling by vehicle but there are many stairs and hills to climb.

A mild headache, nausea, breathlessness and slight dizziness are the 'normal' symptoms of altitude. Many people find it hard to sleep, and alchohol and smoking are best avoided.

There is a pharmaceutical aid to acclimatisation which seems to work. Diamox is a sulphur-based diarrectic, generically termed Acetazolamide. A minor side effect is tingling of the fingers and toes and increased urination.

Dr Shlim suggests that 125mg dosages morning and night are sufficient (just break a 250mg tablet in half). Begin them two mornings before flying to Lhasa and continue for 2 days after arriving in Lhasa. If driving from Nepal, begin taking Diamox the morning that you leave Kathmandu.

In serious cases, pulmonary or cerebral edema leads to unconciousness and can even result in death. The only known cure is to descend to lower altitudes. Symptoms vary: drowsiness, shortness of breath, loss of appetite, severe headaches, acute nausea and disorientation.

It may take several days for symptoms to develop. Take aspirin for the headache and refrain from going higher until the symptoms disappear. If they do not, you must drop to a lower altitude.

Medical kit: Carry a small kit containing these items: Diamox, to help your body acclimatise; Norfloxacin or Ciprofloxacin tablets for diarrhoea; a broad spectrum antibiotic suitable for chest infections; iodine purification tablets for suspect drinking water; plasters; antiseptic cream; throat lozenges; electrolytic powders for energy boosts; eye drops; nasal spray; aspirin.

Hospitals

While major towns have hospitals, the facilities are basic and treatment may include Western pharmaceutical or Chinese herbal remedies (or both). Most doctors speak only Chinese so take your guide or a translator to the hospital with you.

Lhasa: People's Hospital of the Tibetan Autonomous Region, Dzuk Trun Lam, tel: 22353; Tibetan Medicine Hospital of the Tibetan Autonomous Region, Yutok Lam, tel: 23231. The Holiday Inn Lhasa has a doctor on call.

Tsetang: The hospital is located at the western entrance to the town.

Shigatse: The hospital is about 500m (1,600ft) north of the Xigaze Hotel on the same side of the same road.

Shegar: The hospital is 500m (1,600ft) down the same road as the Shegar Guest House, but on the opposite side.

Tibetan Medicine

Traditional Tibetan medicine is a highly evolved science using ayurvedic and herbal techniques based on a combination of traditional Indian and Chinese practices. Evolved in monasteries over centuries and illustrated with *thangkas*, these ancient methods are attracting much international interest.

Security

Tibetans are generally honest and hotel staff can be trusted not to walk off with your belongings. Pickpockets and purse snatchers are virtually unknown and there are few scams aimed at parting you from your money. With more Chinese migrants coming in though, things may change.

While the situation has eased and Tibetans no longer risk being punished for talking with foreigners, be aware that there are still Chinese plainclothes policemen around; temper your comments accordingly. Avoid photographing Chinese soldiers.

Emergency Repairs

Shoe repairmen and other craftsmen can undertake simple sewing and other repairs but count on having to fix it yourself or take it home for repair and plan your packing list accordingly.

COMMUNICATIONS AND NEWS

Post

Postal services are slow and items often go missing. It is best to give your letters or postcards to a fellow traveller to mail in a major city like Guangzhou or Beijing.

Telecommunications

There are telephone services between Lhasa and Tsetang, Gyantse and Shigatse and within each of these towns. The main Post Office and the Telecommunications Building in Lhasa has IDD telephone and fax services. US telephone credit cards are not in use yet.

The Holiday Inn Lhasa offers IDD telephone communications via satellite with most countries, but it costs considerably more. The Holiday Inn Lhasa Hotel offers fax and telex services, and IDD phone cards can be purchased at its reception desk.

News Media

All newspapers are printed in Tibetan or Chinese and there are no foreign English-language publications available.

Chinese television presents a short news programme in English at 10pm every evening. If you carry a shortwave radio, you can listen to BBC and VoA.

USEFUL INFORMATION

Photography

Tibet is an easy yet a frustrating realm to photograph. The sun is so bright, the colours so rich and the contrasts so sharp that any subject becomes a masterpiece.

The contrast between exterior and interior (and sunshine and shadow) is considerable and will affect your choice of film. For most outdoor shots, the light is so bright that even with a film ASA of 25, you will still be shooting at 5.6 at 125th and above. It is best to underexpose to give better light saturation. You can accomplish the same thing by setting your ASA meter one notch higher, ie shooting ASA 100 film at ASA 125.

Building interiors, however, are dimly lit by small, usually quite dirty windows, and candles, a challenge for any camera's metering system. The film you use for exteriors is just not up to it. Carrying a second camera body with a more sensitive film is one answer; a flash is another.

The thin air increases the amount of ultraviolet radiation so that a UV or a skylight filter is a must. At midday, use a warming filter like a light brown 81A. A polarising filter can have a stunning effect on clouds.

Tibet's dust is so fine that it penetrates virtually any closed container. Carry a plastic bag to store your camera equipment when you are not using it. A lens brush, lens cleaning fluid and tissue are useful.

Cameras and camera batteries are not designed to cope with extreme cold and you may find your camera malfunctioning. If it happens during a crucial shot, pull the batteries from the camera, and then rub them on your pants to warm them. Between shots, keep the camera under your jacket next to your body.

USEFUL ADDRESSES

Travel Agents in Tibet

CHINA INTERNATIONAL TRAVEL SERVICE (CITS)
Holiday Inn Lhasa
Tel: 24173

TIBET INTERNATIONAL SPORTS TRAVEL
Himalaya Hotel
Tel: 22293

LHASA TRAVEL COMPANY
Sunlight Hotel
Tel: 22853

CHINESE WORKERS TRAVEL SERVICE
Room 1104, Holiday Inn Lhasa
Tel: 24285
Fax: 34472
Telex: 68025 WTBL CN
Mr G T Sonam, General Manager

Travel Agents in Kathmandu

ADVENTURE TRAVEL NEPAL PVT LTD
P.O. Box 3989
Lazimpath, Kathmandu, Nepal
Tel: 415995, 412906
Fax: 414075

CHO-OYU TREKKING PVT LTD
P.O. Box 4515
Lazimpath, Kathmandu, Nepal
Tel: 418890
Fax: 418390

MOUNTAIN TRAVEL NEPAL PVT LTD
P.O. Box 170
Lazimpath, Kathmandu, Nepal
Tel: 414508, 413019
Fax: 414075, 415659

NEPAL TRAVEL AGENCY PVT LTD
Durbar Marg
Kathmandu, Nepal
Tel: 413188, 412899
Fax: 419003

TIBET TRAVELS AND TOURS PVT LTD
P.O. Box 1397
Thamel, Kathmandu, Nepal
Tel: 212130, 228986
Fax: 415126

YETI TRAVELS PVT LTD
Durbar Marg
Kathmandu, Nepal
Tel: 221234, 222329
Fax: 226153

Travel Agents in Hong Kong

ABERCROMBIE & KENT LTD
27th Floor
Tai Sang Commercial Building
24–34 Hennessy Road
Wanchai, Hong Kong
Tel: 2865 7818
Fax: 2866 0556

CHINA TIBET QOMOLUNGMA TRAVEL LTD
Room 802, Corcodile House
50 Connaught Road
Central, Hong Kong
Tel: 2541 8896

CONCORDE TRAVEL LTD
1st Floor and 7th Floor
8–10 On Lan Street
Central, Hong Kong
Tel: 2526 3391
Fax: 2845 0485

MERA TRAVEL LTD
Room 1307–8 Argyll Centre Phase 1
688 Nathan Road
Kowloon, Hong Kong
Tel: 2391 6892
Fax: 2735 5873

SILKWAY TRAVEL LTD
610–612 Tower 1, Silvercord
30 Canton Road, Tsimshatsui
Kowloon, Hong Kong
Tel: 2724 0888

SWIRE TRAVEL LTD
2nd Floor, Swire House
9 Connaught Road
Central, Hong Kong
Tel: 2844 8482
Fax: 28459182

Diplomatic Missions

Royal Nepal Embassy: Gyatso Tou Lam (opposite the northern wall of the Norbulingka Palace), Lhasa. Tel: 22880. Open Monday–Friday 9.30am–12.30pm.

Government Offices

Public Security Bureau, Dzuk Trun Lam, Lhasa. Tel: 23170.
Immigration Dept, Dzuk Trun Lam, Lhasa. Tel: 23170

Airline Offices

China Southwestern Airlines (CSWA), Mi Mang Lam, Lhasa. Tel: 22417, 23772.
Royal Nepal Airlines, contact the CSWA office in Lhasa.

Banks

Lhasa: Bank of China, Dzuk Trun Lam. Tel: 22796.
Shigatse: Bank of China, Main road. Tel: 2931
Zhangmu: Bank of China, Main road.

FURTHER READING

There are Chinese bookstores in Lhasa but selection is limited. The best-stocked is the **Penchung Kang Bookstore** on Mi Mang Lam Road. Tel: 23249. You will find a better selection of books at bookstores in Kathmandu.

General

Ali, Salim. *Field Guide to the Birds of the Eastern Himalaya*. Oxford University Press. Delhi, 1896 (1977).
David-Neel, Alexandra. *My Journey to Lhasa*. Virago Press, London, 1986. The adventures of Europe's redoubtable female explorer.
Hackett, Peter H. *Mountain Sickness Prevention, Recognition and Treatment*. The American Alpine Club, New York. A valuable, easy-to-carry booklet for off-trail trekkers.
McCue, Gary. *Trekking in Tibet: A Traveler's Guide*. The Mountaineers. Seattle, Washington, 1991. A complete guide to trekking in Central Tibet.
Mierow, Dorothy, and Shrestha, Tirtha Bahadur. *Himalayan Flowers and Trees*. Sahayogi Prakashan, Kathmandu, 1978.

Culture

Berry, Scott. *A Stranger in Tibet, Adventures of a Wandering Zen Monk*. Konansha International, Tokyo and New York,

1989. A well-researched account of th life of Japanese monk Kawaguchi Eka who travelled overland through Tibet i the early 1900s.
Richardson, Hugh. *Adventures of a Tibeta Fighting Monk*. Tamarind Press, Bang kok, 1986. An entertaining and highl informative look at the life of a youn, farm boy who progresses from a herds man to a warrior monk in the 1950s.

History

Avedon, John F. *In Exile from the Lan of Snows*. Vintage Books, New York 1986. The story of the 14th Dala Lama's last days in Tibet and of hi tortuous escape to India.
Fleming, Peter. *Bayonets to Lhasa*. Oxfor University Press. Hong Kong, 1987 Account by Ian Fleming's brother o the Younghusband expedition of 1904

Literature and Religion

Fourteenth Dalai Lama. *Freedom in Exile The autobiography of the Dalai Lama* Hodder and Soughton, London. 1990 Includes much of his earlier biograph and brings followers up to date.
David-Neel, Alexandra. *Tibetan Tale o Love and Magic*. Rupa & Co., Calcutta 1988. Tale of a notorious highwayman married to a demoness who sees the er ror of his ways and turns to Buddhism
Hyde-Chambers, Fredrick & Audrey *Tibetan Folk Tales*. Shambhala, Boulder, Colorado & London, 1981. Includes the tale of Gesar, folk hero of Tibet.
Dowman, Keith. *The Power Places o Central Tibet: The Pilgrim's Guide* Routledge & Kegan Paul, London, 1988. An examination of Tibetan monasteries and the network of supernatura power.

GLOSSARY

ani	nun
bodhisattva	one who has reached enlightenment and who has been reborn to help others
chorten	stupa or chaitya, small shrine sometimes containing a reliquary
deyang	plaza
dharma	Buddhist doctrine, literally 'the path'
dorje	ritual thunderbolt, symbolising indestructability, also called vajra
drokba	nomadic herder
dzong	castle, fortress
gelong	a fully ordained monk
geshe	monk who has attained the highest degree of learning
gompa	monastery
kata	white ceremonial scarf for offering
karma	the cause and effect chain of actions from one life to another
la	mountain pass
lam	road
lama	highly respected religious teacher or elder
lhakhang	chapel, temple or inner sanctuary, literally 'residence of the god'
losar	Tibetan new year
mandala	a symbolic, graphic representation of a tantric deity's realm of existence
phodrang	palace
phurba	ritual dagger
rinpoche	reincarnate head of a monastery, literally 'Precious One'
thangka	a religious painted or embroided scroll
trapa	student or novice monk
tsampa	roasted barley flour

ACKNOWLEDGMENTS

Photography by	**Gary McCue** *and* **David Allardice**
14, 21, 29, 31, 38, 40, 41T, 47, 49B, 50B, 53B, 54T, 67B, 69B, 70B, 88B, 92	
Backcover, 18, 19, 28, 39T, 41B 46T, 58, 60T, 71, 96T	**Craig Lovell**
15, 49T, 54B, 56T, 56B, 59, 61 68, 69T, 84B	**Jock Montgomery**
10, 30B, 45, 51, 62, 63T, 70T, 81, 82, 83, 84T, 85, 87M, 95, 97, 100	**Steve Van Beek**
12, 37, 55, 64, 67T, 86, 87B, 89	**Hans Höfer**
Cover, 74, 75B, 76T, 77T, 77B, 78, 90	**V. Barl**
73, 80, 98, 99	**Steven Powers**
4/5, 8/9	**Lyle Lawson**
76B	**Robin Bradshaw**
16	**Royal Geographical Society**
Handwriting	**V. Barl**
Cover Design	**Klaus Geisler**
Cartography	**Berndtson & Berndtson**

My thanks and appreciation to all those who helped me with this book: Amanu, Dipendra Basnet, Champa, John Frederick, Golma, Gary McCue, Dr David Shlim, G T Sonam, Mark and Jeannette Waites.

Index

P Q R

S T U

W Y Z